MW01165517

Lighting
The
Way Home

The City Rescue Mission Of
Saginaw's First Hundred Years

Gary D. Warner

Lighting the Way Home: The City Rescue Mission of Saginaw's First Hundred Years / by Gary D. Warner

© 2005 City Rescue Mission of Saginaw

All rights reserved. No part of this book may be reproduced, stored in a retrieval system, or transmitted in any form or by any means—electronic, mechanical, photocopy, recording, or otherwise—without written permission of the publisher, except for brief quotations in printed reviews.

Published by City Rescue Mission of Saginaw, MI

Printed in the U.S.A. by TBF Graphics, Saginaw

www.rescuesaginaw.org

Quotations, source information and photos from the *The Saginaw News* and its previous identities, i.e. *The Saginaw Evening News, The Saginaw Courier Herald, The Saginaw News Courier* and *The Saginaw Daily News* © 1905, 1906, 1907, 1908, 1909, 1910, 1911, 1912, 1914, 1918, 1921, 1926, 1930, 1932, 1934, 1935, 1938, 1940, 1943, 1948, 1951, 1952, 1953, 1954, 1955, 1959, 1966, 1969, 1976 The Saginaw News. All rights reserved. Reprinted with permission.

ISBN 0-9773503-0-4

Cover design, art, photography (front, back-top), and typography layout by Gary D. Warner

Pages 113, 120, 132, 139, 143 photography by Dale Wieck

There's no place like home . . .
        Unless you don't have one.

Prologue

Twenty years ago, when I began looking for information about the early days of the Saginaw Rescue Mission, I didn't know I would get hooked on history. As a kid I was like so many of my peers who found the subject to be fairly blasé and I'm sure my grades reflected this view. Mere facts and data can be rather sterile unless you understand them as clues and connections to life in its abundance today. For me it has taken living a bit beyond youth and foolishness to gain an appreciative perspective of past events as shapers of the present.

According to rumor, forty-five years ago roughly, something happened at the Mission that is fairly common in countless establishments. Apparently in a fell stroke of housecleaning,

someone exercised efficiency to a fault and
summarily pitched the old files. Lamentably,
irreplaceable records of the Rescue Mission's
legacy vanished. Thankfully, a few precious items
managed to survive, such as news clippings, but
many of these lacked a date.

Thus my quest for the Mission's heritage would
prove to be a daunting challenge. I had one clue
to initiate my task—the date the Mission opened.
Armed with that single fact, I started scanning
microfilm at Hoyt Library where all the old issues
of the Saginaw News are stored. I hit pay dirt.
The downside of investigating this source is that
prior to 1947, no indexing of any kind exists under
which a subject can be researched. When even
dates of events are unknown, searching is a time
consuming, virtually blind pursuit. If you can
picture sitting in front of a monitor as hundreds of
newspaper pages scroll slowly by, then you may
understand why several times I caught myself
dozing off, even as I held the button down.

Ten years ago, we began to make a few general
appeals to Mission friends who might by chance
be in possession of memorabilia. There was little
response, however, one item surfaced that is now
held as a priceless treasure. It is a single copy of
the Mission's Second Annual Report and it is no

mere collection of typewritten, mimeographed pages. It is a handsome, fascinating booklet with many photographs. Needless to say, it has provided an important bridge across the unknown void. Excerpts and photos from that publication, included in this book, open windows on the past not seen since those days.

A dream starts with a spark that ignites a passion. Just before I finally began drafting this text in earnest, because we still stood in want of much more information, I honestly experienced an almost sickening fear that the book you now hold might not come to fruition. Time was ticking away and I knew I could hold out no longer. As I plunged in I became increasingly excited at how much I was able to garner from the few short stacks of material amassed. I also took comfort in the realization that through all the annals of history, no account is complete because many facts are forever irretrievable—and the extant records are subject to change as new discoveries are made. Accordingly, portions of Mission history offered in past issues of *Vision* are expanded upon and corrected here.

The Rescue Mission is a manifold, relational ministry of both entering in and reaching out. Therefore I have attempted to relate the story globally, particularly in context with Saginaw's past. By way of commitment to historical accuracy, I refrain from conjecture, except for some minor extrapolation of known facts. A few instances of speculation are clearly identified as such.

May the fire of the dream help to brighten the way home.

Gary David Warner
July 2005

Contents

"For I was hungry and you gave me food . . . thirsty and you gave me drink . . . a stranger and you invited me in." Matthew 25:35.

Chapter 1

To the Rescue

Who Are the Needy?

At the heart of it, the word rescue indicates crisis. Really though, this is the true condition of all mankind lost in sin, and the reason God designed a plan of salvation. His coming to earth as God, yet as one of us, together with the work He accomplished on our behalf, is the ultimate rescue mission.

But the ministry called rescue over the last couple of centuries has consistently been linked with people caught in circumstances of acute difficulty: the disadvantaged, the homeless, the drifter. When looking into the history however, you typically find that the people who rose to become the rescue movement's most influential leaders were once in desperate straits themselves, and on the brink of destruction.

Such was the case with Mel Trotter, whose life is a most apt illustration of the old expression about evangelism being 'one beggar telling another beggar where to find bread.' His path toward suicide was intercepted by Tom Mackey, an ex-jockey and card shark.[1] With the compassion of Jesus, he brought Mel into a rescue mission where he would hear the Good News of God's redemptive power. Utterly transformed, from that day forward he passionately sought out others to snatch from the gutters with the same practical lovingkindness he had received.

The metamorphosis God fashioned in the lives of rescue's early leaders was often so dramatic, and so many lost souls were retrieved from ruin as a result, that revival broke out. Hence the rescue mission became a powerful tool of evangelism and an important agent of positive influence in the community. This is the very nature of the background and fertile soil from which the City Rescue Mission of Saginaw sprang and grew.

The rescue mission has always stood as an evangelistic arm of the church reaching out to the neediest element of society. The plight of the destitute may be the result of random circumstances of misfortune, or poor upbringing and bad choices that have led to a lifestyle of crisis. Thus the rescue mission has always had occasion to serve folks from *all* walks of life. No matter the personal status, as the Author of impartial compassion and unconditional love, Jesus is the model of meeting people at the point of their need, and fulfilling them. Furthermore, when encountering someone who is needy, it is incumbent upon God's children to equate that person to Christ Himself.

"Whatever you have done for the least of these my brethren, you have done for Me."   —Jesus

Matthew 25:40

Chapter 2

The Birth of a Phenomenon

The City Rescue Mission of Saginaw traces its roots to a movement that began some eight decades before this local ministry came into being. The phenomenon of the rescue mission was born amidst the first half of the nineteenth century. It was a time of great poverty and distress in the city of Glasgow, Scotland. Acquiring an early passion to spread God's Word, a youngster named David Nasmith had begun distributing Bibles at the age of fourteen. Later, as an adult, he observed that the churches of Glasgow were situated in the midst of some of the poorest neighborhoods, yet were

having little impact. His vision was an
interdenominational agency that would work
alongside churches, providing
for the spiritual and material
welfare of the needy. Thus
the world's first rescue
mission was founded in
1826.[1] The work that
Nasmith established was to
become a model for the birth
of missions in London and
other cities in the United

David Nasmith

Kingdom, Europe, Australia and America. Today
this Christian outreach continues and prospers in
bringing practical help and spiritual hope to the
homeless and disadvantaged people of Glasgow.

First Rescue Missions in America

Self-described as a "rogue and a river thief," the
founder of America's first rescue mission was born
again while reading the Bible during his
confinement in Sing Sing Prison in the 1860s.
Following his release, Jerry McAuley married
Maria. Together, in 1872, the couple opened the
"Helping Hand for Men" on Water Street in New
York City. It was the first religious facility in
America to open its doors to the needy every night
of the year. Later it was called the McAuley Water

Street Mission and today is known as the New York City Rescue Mission.[2]

Other famous mission works that began in the early days of the American movement include the Bowery Mission in the skid row district of New York's lower east side. The Pacific Garden Mission in Chicago was converted from what was called the Pacific Beer Garden. Famed evangelist Dwight L. Moody had suggested the name change to Mission founder, Colonel George Clarke. Today this Mission is renowned for its long running radio drama series, *Unshackled!* that relates stories of lives transformed in Christ.[3] The Union Rescue Mission in Los Angeles began by taking to the streets in 'Gospel Wagons' offering food, clothing and salvation to the less fortunate. During its first sixteen years over 500 people a day were served from temporary sites, and tents were erected for nightly revival

Jerry McAuley

Maria McAuley

meetings. A permanent home was then secured and today the Union Rescue Mission is the nation's largest.

Today throughout America's inner cities some 300 rescue missions minister to the needy. Most of these are affiliated with the **Association of Gospel Rescue Missions** established in 1913. The organization facilitates fellowship and cooperation among its member missions worldwide—uniting and advancing their effectiveness in redeeming the lives of homeless and needy people.

Chapter 3

Rescue's Champion

No one could have imagined the miraculous turn of events that would follow the ragged bum who staggered into Chicago's Pacific Garden Mission on January 19, 1897. Knocking over chairs as he entered, he was so drunk that he couldn't even come up with his name.[1] Unemployed, broke, unkempt and wearing little clothing, a cruel snow storm that night had pummeled his already despondent soul to absolute hopelessness. He had even sold the shoes off his feet to buy one final drink before an intended lethal plunge into the icy waters of Lake Michigan. God however, had other plans.

Melvin Ernest Trotter,[2] was born May 16, 1870, one of three sons and four daughters of William and Emily Trotter. The boys all followed dad's footsteps tending bar and becoming alcoholics. Mel, however, learned to barber at age 17. After moving away from home, he was drinking heavily by age 19, gambling, and losing his job as a result. He somehow managed, for a time, to keep his problems hidden from Lottie Fisher, the girl he married in 1891. Shocked and heartbroken, she pleaded with Mel to give up drinking. He would honor her by succeeding in becoming sober, at least for a matter of weeks, then return to drunken binges. Slowly, the vicious cycle would spiral Mel evermore helplessly downward.

Soon he was committing burglaries to support his worsening addiction. He was hospitalized and treated for alcoholism, but before fifteen minutes could pass following his discharge, he sold the medicine kit he'd been given for the price of three drinks of whiskey.

In the wake of one ten-day bender, Trotter returned home to find his wife holding the lifeless body of their two-year-old son. Bitterly remorseful, he embraced Lottie before the child's white casket and vowed he would never touch liquor again as long as he lived. Two hours after the funeral, he stumbled home so drunk he couldn't see.

Mel was 27 on that bitter January night in Chicago when he had given up all hope of changing his life for the better. Serving as a doorman, Tom Mackey urged him inside and helped him to a seat against a wall so that he wouldn't fall over. At the pulpit was Harry Monroe, a converted alcoholic who had become Superintendent of the Pacific Garden Mission. Observing Trotter's desperate condition, he asked the crowd to bow with him as he prayed, "O God, save that poor, poor boy." Monroe then testified of being saved at age 27 after wandering into the Mission some seventeen years earlier. At the close of the service, Mel walked forward and Monroe led him to Christ.

Harry Monroe

From the moment of his conversion, he was free of the desire for alcohol and never touched it again. He soon found a barbering job and then sent for his wife. During his first year as a Christian, he memorized 365 verses of Scripture. His favorite was II Corinthians 5:17 because God indeed transformed him into a new creation.[3] He began telling practically

everyone he met about the Lord including nearly
every drifter in the street. He spent every night at
the Mission, singing and testifying. Thus he became
known as 'the man who raved about Jesus.'

When the City Rescue Mission of Grand Rapids
was preparing to open in 1900, founder Harry
Monroe tapped Mel Trotter to head up the work as
superintendent. Not only had he no experience as
such, he had never so much as led a mission meeting.

People of every stripe packed the first service
on opening night but the crowd was predominantly
made up of women. Mel was so petrified when he
got up to preach that he didn't seem to realize he
was speaking in his former street slang. Nevertheless,
when he gave the invitation, several ladies trusted
Christ and were permanently changed. One became
a missionary, one married a preacher, and one
became a regular participant in Mission activities.

Within a few months a powerful revival broke
out with between two and twenty-five souls
coming to know the Lord each night. Among
them was Mel's brother, George. In fact, some
1500 conversions were recorded during the first
year of ministry. Under Mel's forty-year-long
leadership the Mission continued to prosper and
expand and is thriving to this day. He also led the

great revival of Grand Rapids in 1919 and went on
to lead many other area-wide revivals.

Mel Trotter genuinely cared about people.
Compassion flowed from him and when it did,
people knew it was the love of Christ Himself that
touched them. Adopting the motto, *Everlastingly
At It*, his burden for the lost seemed boundless and
his drive unflagging as he was led to other cities.
Even when suffering physically, Mel was not one
to allow illness and its weakening effects hamper
his labors for the Lord.[4] Then again, as a manager,
he was extraordinarily adept at knowing how to
get work done through other people. Both of his
brothers, George and Will became active in rescue
work and helped Mel organize missions throughout
America. The faithful prayers of Emily Trotter
resulted in the salvation of all the men in her life,
one by one, beginning with son Will, then Mel,
George, and finally husband William.

As an evangelist, Mel regularly took part in the
campaigns of R. A. Torrey and Billy Sunday. His
testimony thrilled multitudes and inspired the
establishment of still more missions, many with
his assistance. Mel's work in 54 Army YMCA
camps over a period of twenty months during
World War I resulted in 15,000 conversions.
Availing himself of this opportunity required the

George Trotter   *Will Trotter*

satisfaction of an entertainment clause in the allies' contract with the YMCA. So he organized the American Four Quartet and featured them in the work. They went on to travel the U.S. ministering in Bible conferences and evangelistic campaigns, including the Billy Sunday crusades. One of the group's member vocalists, Thomas Hinkin, later became a long time superintendent of the Saginaw Rescue Mission.[5]

The American Four Quartet. Tom Hinkin is standing second from left. Mel Trotter is seated at right.

The name of Mel Trotter therefore figures prominently in the history of the rescue movement. Harry Monroe taught him how to develop and oversee a mission. Thus Mel cut his teeth in Chicago and gained his legs in Grand Rapids. Then in franchise-like fashion, he set about replicating the rescue mission with its various features everywhere he could. God blessed his efforts because while the *objective* was planting missions, the *goal* was winning souls to Christ. Although the patterning was consistent, the Spirit of God would make each mission as unique as all of His creations. As a matter of fact, the City Rescue Mission of Saginaw was the very first of some 67 missions Mel was responsible for establishing across the United States.[6] Bathed in prayer, his method of sustaining and developing them was accomplished through men he had discipled and thoroughly trained, just as Harry Monroe did with him. Thus Mel's life and work could succinctly be epitomized as, *born again to reproduce*. While we certainly cannot all be Mel Trotters, shouldn't the same be said of all God's children.

Over the course of his wide ministry activity, the *ol' man*—as he preferred being called—continued to head the work in Grand Rapids. Despite suffering ill health during the last few years of his life, Mel remained as active in the ministry as possible. His funeral on September 14, 1940 was held in Grand Rapids at the Mission that would henceforth bear his name. Among the speakers was his eminent friend, Dr. Harry A. Ironside, pastor of the Moody Memorial Church, Chicago.

Mel Trotter
Founder, City Rescue Mission of Saginaw

Chapter 4

A
Wide-Open
Opportunity

It could well be said that in many ways, the 1800s was a time of adolescence for the new nation called the United States of America. It was a time of tremendous expansion. From east to west, new communities sprang up, but law and especially order were usually not well-developed features until much later. In this sense Saginaw was typical of many frontier towns.

Following the Civil War, the lumber industry became America's largest employer. Michigan had risen rapidly as the nation's foremost producer of lumber. Saginaw was booming, and literally became the undisputed lumber capitol of the world.[1] Scores of giant sawmills lined its timber-jammed River. Immigrants by the tens of thousands filled plentiful jobs. In point of fact, Michigan's magnificent white pine, nicknamed "green gold," produced far more wealth than the western gold rush. It's a challenge to come up with an adequate explanation as to why the latter has received so much greater attention in history books. Perhaps the intrigue of unearthing the elusive precious metal held more glamour than the sawing of ubiquitous trees.

Unfortunately, the excitement accompanying the timber boom's grand prosperity led to greed. Intermingle self-indulgence with the general lack of law and order and you have a natural breeding ground for corruption.

Lumberjacks led a lonely life working northern forests for up to six months—straight through the winter. Bosses learned the hard way that women, cards and liquor only interfered with timber harvesting, so all three were banned from the camps. When spring finally arrived, thawing rivers carried the annual log drive to the mills. Saginaw then was *the* place to go, so trainloads of 'shanty boys' came swarming through the Potter Street station by the thousands. After the long, hard, isolated winter, the throng dubbed the "Red Sash Brigade" was primed *full tilt* for a break, and merchants were more than eager to profit from the patronage.

All the high-spirited energy created a carnival of carnality. Consequently, the city acquired a most infamous reputation for being *wide-open.* Both Saginaw, and Bay City with its darksome Catacombs, were notorious as wild places where men could indulge their senses in as much wanton excess as they could stomach. Orgies of drinking, womanizing, and brutal brawling became legend. Lumberjacks would build up so much anticipation for a furlough in *Timbertown* that they referred to their passage as a "ticket to hell." Like so many communities in earlier days, carrying a concealed weapon was legal, as was prostitution.[2] In fact, the 'oldest profession' was considerably more prevalent in the lumber towns than in the western cow towns and mining settlements. Over 200 saloons once dominated Saginaw's east side alone. Most of them employed at least several women of 'easy virtue' in order to be successful. It was Tilden Street (Water Street today) that was dubbed

White Row, a hotbed of unsavory enterprises, yet it was said that brothels flourished throughout the city. About a fourth of violent deaths were associated in some way with prostitution.

Rampant hedonism notwithstanding, upright, decent society did exist. However, Saginaw historian, Stuart Gross wrote:

> One of the nagging questions that emerges from reading about these "good old days" is the absence of the church in protesting the evils in such places as the Catacombs. There may have been some, but I can't point to any instance where the ministers banded together and cried in unison "enough!" There may be a reason. Lumber barons and the leading merchants did go to church. It was the proper thing to do. These rich men probably were the main support of churches, and ministers may have been fearful of losing that support if they protested from the pulpit or attempted to organize a movement to clean up the saloons. The timber towns were wild and almost lawless because the leaders of the day wanted it that way. There can be no other conclusion.[3]

Before the turn of the century, clear cutting had utterly decimated Michigan's primeval forests, from the Saginaw and Muskegon Rivers to the Straits of Mackinaw. Hence the decline of the great timber boom was consummated. It's related avarice and decadence however, persisted in holding sway over *the fallen,* enslaved by prurient passions.[4]

Chapter 5
Ripe for Rescue

In 1905, Theodore Roosevelt presided over the Union's forty-five states.[1] Despite the worst flood to devastate the local area the previous year, Saginaw was slowly recovering from the lumber era's demise. Cutover lands were being farmed and the city was becoming a diverse center of manufacturing. Automobiles were a novelty— there were only a about a hundred on the city's streets.[2] By day, downtown Saginaw was a bustling hub of respectable commerce. By night, said the Saginaw Evening News, "the fallen . . . swarm Tilden Street . . ." [3]

In the aftermath of the depravity linked with the timber boom, the streets of Saginaw were thus

teeming with wayward, needy souls in want of
redemption, so much that many Christians did
indeed unite to say "enough"—by praying for the
establishment of a rescue mission. Clearly, it was a
ministry whose time had come—amidst a mission
field ripe for harvest. Paradoxically, it was A. C.
White, an honorable, post boom Saginaw lumber
magnate, who sought the help of the renowned
Mel Trotter, Superintendent of the City Rescue
Mission of Grand Rapids.[4] Trotter later recalled,

> As our Grand Rapids mission grew, naturally
> the converts spread out through all the State
> and beyond. Other cities asked for the
> establishment of a mission. We first went to
> Saginaw. I just took a bunch of our fellows over
> one Sunday. In the morning we put on a
> meeting in the different churches, giving our
> testimonies; how the Lord had saved us in the
> Mission. In the afternoon and evening we were
> in the big auditorium, where we raised enough
> money to open a mission.[5]

It was Sunday, October 22nd and among the five
men with Mel that day was William Van Domelen,
who would later serve out his life as the
Superintendent of the Muskegon Rescue Mission.
Indeed, the work was efficiently organized, with
$1,600, a large sum for the time, cheerfully

pledged as seed money. Mel would present his brother, George W. Trotter, as candidate for first Superintendent. He was chosen unanimously. Vacating his post at the helm of a mission in St. Paul, Minnesota, the Trotter family moved to Saginaw. Preparations began in earnest, support grew rapidly, and within three weeks the work was poised for launch. Dan W. Bush[6] would serve as Assistant Superintendent followed by Ray Bird.[7] Dan was saved at the Mission in Grand Rapids and his story is the subject of a chapter in the book, *These Forty Years* by Mel Trotter. Mrs. George Trotter would have charge of outreach to the poor.

The Door is Opened

The date was *11/11* at the address of *111* Genesee[*] Avenue, and on page *11*, column *1*,[†] the Saginaw Evening News announced the opening of the City Rescue Mission. Adjoining Saginaw's seamy White Row district, the site's selection was both a bold stroke of strategy and appropriate irony. This first Rescue Mission facility was reportedly converted from among the many saloons of the immediate area. There was even one right next door, and for a time, a saloon flanked the Mission on the left as well.[8]

---

[*]East Genesee today.
[†]The repeated appearance of the numeral '1' in connection with the Mission's founding is undoubtedly an insignificant fluke (unless one considers the chronology of rescue missions founded by Mel Trotter). Still, it is an interesting coincidence.

THE SAGINAW EVENING NEWS.

SAGINAW, MICH., SATURDAY, NOVEMBER 11, 1905

RESCUE MISSION OPENS TONIGHT

MOTTO OF MOVEMENT IS "WHOSOEVER WILL MAY COME" — ATTRACTING MUCH ATTENTION.

Saginaw's first City Rescue Mission will open its doors to "whosoever will come" at 111 Genesee avenue tonight.   The founding of the mission has been something long hoped for by many Christian people of this city, and, now that one is started, it is receiving very close attention.

In speaking to The News Saturday morning, Superintendent George Trotter, said that the location of the mission right near the heart of the business district where thousands of people pass daily is ideal.   One-eleven was formerly a saloon, dingy and dark.   Now it is as clean and bright a room as can be found. The walls have been repapered attractively, the ceiling is fresh under a coat of new paint and an entire new hardwood floor has been put in.   At the rear of the spacious room is a platform, on which is an organ and an altar.   Besides this space there is room for the seating of over 200 people. Behind the platform is an office and coat room and the whole establishment is lighted with a system of fine lights, which will make it bid fair for the name of the "Daylight Mission."

The opening service will be this evening at 7:30 o'clock.   There will be a half hour's song service which is always a great feature of mission work and then there will be several speakers, among them Rev. Emil Montanus of St. John's church, Rev. J. A. Dunkel of the Warren Avenue Presbyterian church and Superintendent Trotter.   Then there will be duets and musical numbers of Miss Miller, Miss Ruth Brady and Miss Jennie Hough. Like services will be given every night in the year, and the meeting time will always be 7:30 o'clock. On the windows of the mission in great letters so that he who runs may read, are printed the words, "Whosoever Will May Come" in white and blue. A background for this lettering is to be made of blood red so that, when the building is lighted at night, the window alone will attract many of the fallen who swarm Tilden street at night. The mission has rented the three floors of the building and, as soon as the second and third floors are repaired, they will also be utilized.

Superintendent and Mrs. Trotter are very enthusiastic in the work. Mr. Trotter was converted several years ago in the mission established and run by his brother, the famous "Mell," in Grand Rapids. From there he went to Los Angeles, Cal., where he did most efficient service, and later was stationed at San Antonio. When a mission was started at St. Paul, Minn., he was placed in charge and served there until now he comes to Saginaw. The mission is noticed by everyone who passes on the street. Saturday morning when it began to take on an appearance of life and cleanliness, many passers, among them some of the most prominent of Saginaw's business men stopped and made the mission a call. This interest is very gratifying to Superintendent Trotter and he says that, from present outlook, the mission has a very bright future. "We've come to save the lost," says he, "and we're going to do it. If they won't come, then we'll go and bring them in. That's the way we work." Open air services will not be held during the winter, but, as soon as spring comes, a gospel wagon will be put on the road. Of the $1,600 pledged, $300 came in during the past week.

111 Genesee Avenue - where the Saginaw Rescue Mission started. Here the building was adorned in observance of Saginaw's Semicentennial, August 1907.

Reaping the Harvest

The impact of the new ministry was felt immediately. By the spring of 1906, after just over four months of operation, the Saginaw Evening News related Superintendent George Trotter's account of the Rescue Mission's resounding triumph:

> The Mission in Saginaw has had remarkable growth and been unusually successful. Superintendent Trotter has worked in St. Paul, Grand Rapids, Los Angeles, and other cities but declares Saginaw has surpassed all in lively interest and starting of the work.[9]

Brother Mel commented, "That Mission was a "hummer" from the beginning . . . My what a fine crowd of folks were converted there."[10] The average nightly attendance of 200 at Mission services was near capacity. There had been 350 conversions. Many of them had been regulars of the Oakley Saloon next door. Nearly every pastor in the city had spoken from the Mission platform.

Also revealed was the Mission's early ministry to women, previously thought by many to have only begun in more recent times. The Mission's

First meeting hall of the Saginaw Rescue Mission, 111 Genesee.

spreading influence was evident from members
added to area churches, "to the brothels on Tilden
Street from which it has taken fallen women and
given them opportunities under which they are
living Christian lives," the News reported. At a
later date the News referred to the Mission as, "a new
feature in the reclaiming work of Saginaw. . ."[11]
Despite an additional $900 expended above the
figure it commenced with, support garnered from
the Mission's recognition in the community
enabled it to handily meet the first year's budget
of $2,500.

THANKFUL FOR THE MISSION.

RAY BIRD.

A YEAR ago the 14th of last October I found my way into the City Rescue Mission, 111 Genesee Ave., and heard of Jesus Christ and His power to save, and the testimony of Supt. Geo. W. Trotter and how Jesus came into his life and saved him from a life of sin. I sat in the house under conviction, and said, if that is true, God helping me, I am going to be a Christian. That night I prayed, God be merciful to me, to me a sinner, and save me for Jesus' sake; and He saved me from all my sin. Thanks be to God.

I was a young man just starting on the downward path of sin. I never drank or used tobacco of any kind in my life, but I had other sins fastened to me that were taking me down to hell. But I laid them all at the feet of Jesus who cleansed me from all sin. Today I am a new creature, old things have passed away, behold, all things are become new.

I do thank God for planting a Rescue Mission in Saginaw, one that is open every night in the week and where Jesus Christ is lifted up. The Rescue Mission is the brightest spot in all Saginaw to me.

Chapter 6

To the Byways

Meeting Human Need in the Name of Jesus

The motto was, *Whosever will may come*, and from the beginning, the Rescue Mission has been a place where those in want could do just that, freely receiving the physical and spiritual assistance so sorely needed. But the staff was not content to merely be headquartered in the work. It didn't occur to them. They actively hit the streets, reaching out to the poor of the community. Mission converts and volunteers partnered with them. Families were clothed and fed. Homes without fathers present received care in the form of delivered baskets of groceries and the provision of heating fuel (coal).[1] As a result, entire

households came to know the Lord. "That's
where Ray Bird found the Lord, also his sister and
his folks," remarked Mel Trotter. "Ray came to
Grand Rapids later on, and worked as my
assistant."[2] Broken families also were restored.
The needy sick received free medical treatment
from Mission board member, Dr. Martha
Longstreet, and from Dr. Edith Hunsberger. Good
homes were found for orphaned and neglected
children. There was also appropriate care and
placement of the elderly. Early in the Mission's
development, a free labor bureau was established to
assist the unemployed in getting back on their feet.[3]
Collectively, these efforts were called relief work.

**Mrs. Robert Allen and Mrs. John DeFore with
children that were placed in St. Vincents's
Orphan Home.**

Granted, the Gospel of salvation was the
overarching emphasis, as intended. But the focus
on relief was nothing less than equally sharp
because Mission staff fully understood that Jesus'
love is synonymous with charity. Hence from the
outset, they had their *ducks in a row*. They sought
to demonstrate and prove Christ's compassion in
every tangible way. Since God's glory is inherent
in such motivation, rather than competing with
other efforts, the Mission sought to cooperate
"with every religious and charitable society in the
city . . . *in dealing with families* [it] *does not
discriminate between any.*"[4]

BOASTED ON HIS MORALITY.

TWO years have passed since the Rescue Mission was organized. The first year found me a scoffer, but thank God the second year finds me a Christian and a worker. I want to say to you that I was a man that boasted on my morality, but if I could get a drink or shake a game of dice when I thought none of my friends were watching me who would tell my wife or any of my church friends, I would do it. But as a result of hearing the plain gospel of Jesus Christ and the testimony of redeemed men at the Mission, February 5th, 1907, I accepted Christ, and I stand to-day a clean-cut Christian man.

JOHN DEFORE.

I have no more desire for drink, for tobacco or for any of the things that are cursing men's lives to-day than if I never knew of them.

I am thankful today because we have a happy Christmas home.

Chapter 7
Lifting the Fallen

Mrs. George Trotter was described as, "the devoted little woman who has chosen to aid her husband in the Mission." The focus of her compassion was especially fixed on Tilden Street's White Row—the most prominent of vice zones[1] and in closest proximity to the Rescue Mission— where myriad unfortunates inhabited shadowy bordellos and sleazy saloons. Tragically, the "women" typically engaged in the abominable trade were but tender young teenagers between the ages of fourteen and sixteen—who had either run away or been turned out of their homes. Claims indicate that some started as young as eleven. Fearful and desperate to survive, they were easy prey for silver-tongued saloonkeepers and "sympathetic" madams who deceptively lured them into renting their bodies for the abusive utility of lecherous consumers.[2] Of girls in these circumstances Mel Trotter said, "They are trapped before they ever suspect it. Then, of course, it seems too late."[3]

No decent lady would dare be caught dead on White Row. Mrs. Trotter however, was compelled by Jesus' example of seeking out sinners over the righteous who knew no need of Him. On a mission of mercy, she regularly made her way along the appalling avenue, entrusting both her reputation and safety to God. Possessed of a holy boldness seemingly devoid of fear, she would march directly into the dens of iniquity to meet the pitiful, fallen girls. Did anyone go with her? One can only imagine both the shock and ire of the proprietors. They were known to take vengeance if a competitor took away one of their girls. Mysteriously, they must have been restrained from retaliation. "The Holy Spirit is a gentlemen," they say. Perhaps in this instance, He employed a tactic of divine intimidation. Meeting each girl eye to eye, the authenticity of Jesus' love shining out from Mrs. Trotter was unmistakable as she shared the wondrous news of God's redemptive power. By the hand, she led many precious young ladies out of darkness into the Light of new Life.

Mrs. George W. Trotter - prepared for an errand of mercy.

Limited records make it difficult to positively confirm exactly when the Rescue Mission formally began emergency lodging and serving prepared meals under its own auspices. Apparently it didn't happen right away. Yet the Second Annual Report declares, "We feed all who are hungry; sleep all who are homeless or without the means of a bed ..."

Regardless, the Saginaw Evening News report
of Mrs. Trotter's work related that she,

> . . . goes into places where women generally
> fear to go, excepting those of the lost . . .
> Her sympathy and charity are of the kind
> Divine and the silent records of the Mission
> show that she has helped many a poor girl in
> trouble to better things and brought out of the
> painted places many women to a higher life.[4]

The Second Annual Report further states,
"Many fallen girls have been cared for and given
good homes." In other words, the girls were taken
under wing, led to salvation and nurtured in
righteousness. Were they able to place each girl
immediately, or was it necessary to lodge them
temporarily at the Mission? If only we could view
those records today!

Mr. and Mrs. George Trotter (second row) with *Some of Our Girls,* as the caption read in the Second Annual Report. (Mrs. Trotter is second from left).

Chapter 8

The Gospel Wagon

A former counterfeiter, Harry Monroe had been won to Christ in 1880 by Colonel Clarke, Superintendent of the Pacific Garden Mission. Soon after, Harry was given charge of the song services and helped bring the Mission hall alive with exuberant singing. He became a master at winning souls to Jesus. He also introduced the idea of the Gospel Wagon. From a horse-drawn vehicle, workers preached, gave testimonies and sang the Gospel to people on the street.[1] The Gospel Wagon became a key outreach instrument of rescue mission work. It likewise became well identified with Moody Bible Institute.[2] Churches and other ministries would utilize it in street evangelism as well.

Billy Sunday, the popular professional baseball player for the Chicago White Sox, first heard the good news of salvation preached by Harry Monroe from the Pacific Garden Mission's Gospel Wagon at the corner of State and Van Buren (Chicago). Visiting the Mission that same night, he liked what he heard and soon thereafter trusted Christ as Lord and Savior.[3] He too acquired a passion to win souls and gained renown as the illustrious *baseball evangelist*. Holding mass crusades across America, he was his era's equivalent of Billy Graham. Whenever Sunday would share his personal testimony and his encounter with the Gospel Wagon he declared, "I never go by that street without thanking God for saving me."[4] Saginaw Rescue Mission founder, Mel Trotter, was associated with Sunday, took part in his evangelistic campaigns and occasionally preached in his stead when Billy was ill. Following her husband's death, Helen Sunday began a speaking ministry and served in rescue missions across the country. "I love them because that's where my Billy was saved," she said. Her dedicated work for over two decades fondly identified her as a *mother* to countless rescue mission workers and converts.[5]

Having played a primary role in its opening,
A. C. White was elected President of the Saginaw
Rescue Mission, heading up its first Board of
Directors. A key figure in Saginaw's new
manufacturing growth, he had successfully
established a vast mill and lumberyards on South
Jefferson Avenue in 1899. He was widely
respected as one of the most influential citizens,
being closely associated with the community's
best interests.[6] Its charitable work firmly
recognized, by midsummer of 1906, the Rescue
Mission was ready to further expand its outreach.
Purchased for $150 and provided as a gift from Mr.
White, the Gospel Wagon was launched on
Sunday, July 15th.[7]

**The Gospel Wagon in front of the Mission at 111 Genesee prepares to
depart for street services. Standing - John DeFore; second to the right
of him - Lanson W. Andrus.**

A man well seasoned in Gospel Wagon work, Edward E. Leary, of the Moody Institute, was brought to town to assist Superintendent George Trotter in establishing the new facet of ministry. (Subsequently, Mr. Leary was called westward to take charge of the City Rescue Mission of Los

 Angeles, a direct affiliate of the Union Rescue Mission).[8] Street services were conducted in the same manner as those held in the Mission hall. The wagon was described as a large vehicle able to seat fifteen people. It's platform

Edward E. Leary   and railing especially suited it for speaking and singing, and it carried an organ. Three services were held each Sunday afternoon in front of the Tower block at Genesee and Lapeer Avenues, on the west side in front of the Court House, and then at the corner of Washington and Genesee.

One man's personal assessment of the new outreach was much like Billy Sunday's. "I truly believe I would this day be in hell had it not been for the blessed Gospel Wagon," he related to Superintendent Trotter. The affirmation was similarly echoed by unnumbered masses in Saginaw.[9]

Circa 1907: Gospel Wagon ministry in the 400 block of Genesee, south side. Second from left aboard the Wagon - Lanson W. Andrus; standing - George Trotter; behind driver - Robert Allen.

Chapter 9

Reaching Further

During the summer, pleasant evenings were taken advantage of by shifting regular services outside, in front of the Mission. This proved to be a smart move as it attracted many more people.

Initiated at the same time as the Gospel Wagon ministry, the Mission began conducting jail services each Sunday morning. Additionally, factory meetings commenced. Opening at the Pere Marquette railroad shops, a service was then held at one of Saginaw's leading industrial plants each Wednesday during the noon hour.[1]

Following Up

Soon, three Bible classes, for men and women separately, were being taught at the Mission. In January 1908, Sunday School began "for the children on our streets."[2] It was held each Sunday afternoon so as not to interfere with other Sunday Schools. Additionally, records affirm that by this time, prepared meals were being served at the Mission.[3]

The Bible class for men formally enrolled those who came to know the Lord under the Mission's ministry. They even elected officers. Although it initially met only once a week and was open to any man, it is safe to look at this class as an early form of today's Discipleship Program. Among positive results within the first six years, as many as a half dozen men went on to seminary and became ministers of the Gospel. Several, including one woman, went into rescue mission careers.[4] At separate times, as it turned out, no less than four of the men were destined to be future superintendents of the Saginaw Rescue Mission.[5]

United We Stand

The cause of the Rescue Mission is a unifying one. Because it has always been interdenominational, it is viewed by the Christian community as an outstretched missionary arm of the church as a whole. Accordingly, the churches have always rallied to it. To our knowledge, the Mission has perpetually enjoyed united support. If any sectarian issues ever existed, they have decidedly taken a back seat under the banners of *No creed but Christ—No law but love*, and *Whosoever will may come.* Down through its history, the wisdom of the plan has thus been proven.

The Greater Blessing of Giving

Jesus said, "Where your treasure is, there will your heart be also." Matthew 6:21. Mission supporters have affirmed the inescapable veracity of this principle from the beginning. Having opened their pocketbooks to the cause, they also gave of themselves as a labor of love. The value of volunteers is literally beyond price, *and* indispensable. In point of fact, a vast volume of ministry would simply never happen without them. The void would stagger the imagination. Not only would the Mission have failed to develop and thrive as it has, it may never have gotten off the ground.

Gripped by a pioneering spirit, Mission friends eagerly joined the cause in whatever appropriate way they could.[6] Many volunteers were Mission

converts, excited to be a part of the ministry that
had rescued them. Reciprocally, they wanted to
help others in the same way.

Knit Together

The Women's Society, a separate ministry from
the later established Mission Auxiliary, was
recognized by 1914.[7] The Society may have
formed much earlier but its inception eludes
pinpointing. It was devoted to numerous efforts,
in particular, mending and organizing clothing for
distribution. Members also visited the sick and
prepared meals served to Mission Bible classes.
Burgeoning industriousness with needle, yarn and
thread would redefine the group as the Mothers
Sewing Circle briefly, and then the Women's
Sewing Society. There was even a junior version of
it known as the Teen Age Girls Sewing Club. By
today's standards their accomplishments were
amazing. Not only were garments repaired, re-
cut, and reassembled, numerous articles were
regularly made from scratch. Creations included
quilts, mittens, coats, baby clothes, dresses and
pants.[8]

Saginaw City Rescue Mission Women's Sewing Society, circa 1930.

The Main Event

Raising financial support for the Mission was a
traditional aspect of the superintendent's regular
duties. To boost these efforts, an inspiring event
was held each year for the purposes of magnifying
the work of the Mission before the public, and
fulfilling the budget.[9] The annual meeting was the
forerunner of today's annual banquet. The first
anniversary was observed in several different
churches at different times. Saginaw Rescue
Mission founder, Mel Trotter, returned to headline
the event as keynote speaker. His associate, the
eminent tenor, Peter Quartel, combined his voice
with Mel's in duet, a feature for which they were
famous.

The second annual meeting was billed as a Big
Rally. The venue was the theater of the once
famous Music Academy. As asked, the various
churches throughout the city suspended their
regular Sunday evening services and youth
fellowships in support of the Mission. Again, Mel
Trotter would speak along with other noteworthy
mission workers who came to town. Peter Quartel
returned to take charge of the music.[10] This
included a mass choir drawn from area churches
and numbering in the hundreds. Singing duet
with Mel Trotter was Pacific Garden Mission

Superintendent, Harry Monroe, the man who led him to Christ. Harry was also a featured speaker. Growing support would necessitate holding future annual events in larger venues such as the Saginaw Auditorium,[11] directly across from the Academy at Washington and Janes Avenues.

The annual meeting would next adopt the title of Homecoming, inviting back all the men and women whose lives were transformed under the Mission's ministry.[12]

Passing the Torch

By the end of April 1908, George Trotter's tenure in Saginaw drew to a close as he answered a call to return to Los Angeles.[13] There he took over the helm of the Union Rescue Mission where his brother, Will, had previously served as Superintendent. Ira L. Eldridge of Grand Rapids, another product of what was informally called the Trotter school of evangelism, would next fill the office of superintendent of

Ira Eldridge

the Saginaw Mission. True to the custom of those days, he was assisted in the 'relief work' by his wife.[14]

As an example of Mission work among families, here is one poignant story that Superintendent Eldridge shared with the public not long after assuming his duties in Saginaw:

Many a pathetic scene meets the eye of the superintendent and his wife in their visits. One home we entered (if it could be called home) was in a down town block where a father and four children were trying to keep house, the mother having died four months previous. The oldest child was 10, a little girl, trying to do the housework and help father care for a sick baby brother 16 months old, with nothing to do [it] with.

Mrs. Eldridge took the baby home with her and cleaned it up, put clean clothing on and called a physician and it was found necessary to perform a slight operation and it was taken to St. Mary's hospital where it will receive proper medical attendance and care. When found the child was in a starving condition. The father had done the best he could under his circumstances, but did not have the money and did not

know how. This is only one of the many
sad cases of misfortune that comes under
our observation.[15]

Eldridge served for approximately two years
after which Robert Allen took over the reins as
Superintendent. He was no stranger to the work
in Saginaw having already been enthusiastically
active since its inception. Once a slave to alcohol,
he was born again just days before the Mission
came into being.[16] Additionally, his wife, who had
worked for two years alongside Mrs. George
Trotter, headed up the relief work.[17]

WHAT A TESTIMONY DID.

ROBT. ALLEN.

Mr. Allen is Car Locomotive foreman of
P. M. at Flint, Mich.

MORE than two years have passed since I accepted Christ as my Savior, When I came to him I was in sin. I drank whiskey and did the other things that go with that kind of a life until I was away down; my character and self respect was gone. I could not support my home, and my wife went to work at different things which she could do to keep the home together.

I heard the testimony of a Rescue Mission man and was brought under conviction of sin, and on the 17th of October, 1905, I came to Christ and told Him if He would take the sins out of my life that were taking me to hell, I would do, be or say anything for Him.

He heard my prayer and saved me from my sins, and since then He has wonderfully blessed me both in my spiritual and temporal life. While I had a wonderful experience then in being set free from whiskey, tobacco and other habits, today my experience is still more wonderful as I know my Savior better and I have been walking and talking with Him ever since.

I praise God that he ever led men to open the Rescue Mission, for what it has done for me has more than paid for all the money that has been expended on it: and what it has done for me it has done for hundreds of others. I always want to study to show myself "Approved unto God, a workman who needeth not to be ashamed, rightly dividing the word of truth."

Chapter 10
Movements of Progress

During its fifth year of ministry, 1910, the Rescue Mission facilities were relocated for the first time. Specific reasons are not clear but the move was made to the 200 block of Germania, now known as Federal Avenue. There is a claim that the Mission was temporarily housed in a tent at the northwest corner of Jefferson and Germania.[1] As best as can be surmised, it may have been during the summer of 1910, until a move could be made into a hall at 217 Germania Avenue.[2]

It is reasonable to consider that each successive move in early days better suited the operation of the ministry as it developed and grew. Naturally, priority has always been placed on keeping the Mission in close proximity to the needy. Thus it has remained within the inner city.

As quickly as the next year, the Mission apparently found it advantageous to move once again. This time it would take over the McColgan building, formerly occupied by the National Cooperative Grocery Company, 223 Lapeer Avenue at Weadock.[3]

Mission facilities would occupy three different locations on Lapeer at four successive times. The next move was roughly a block and a half to the west. For the stated purpose of expanding the Mission's usefulness and convenience, the building leased at 117 would undergo renovations in the fall of 1913.[4] This included an addition to the number of beds for lodging. The building apparently served the Mission well as it remained here for fourteen years when the decision was made to return to the last location.

The Succession of Leadership

People to people. This is how the ministry of the Rescue Mission—meeting human need in the name of Jesus—is accomplished. Whether on the forefront or behind the scenes, no one is unimportant. Even followers lead those coming behind them by example.

Nevertheless, just as the old lighthouse could not function without a "Head Keep," this ministry could not flourish as it has for a century without dedicated leaders. As in any organization, the Rescue Mission's level of effectiveness has typically been commensurate with the effectiveness of the leadership and staff. God's blessing abides as his servants remain submitted and obedient to Him.

The Saginaw Rescue Mission's early years were simultaneous with the burgeoning era of the rescue movement. Consequently, there was a notable turnover in leadership locally, especially through a fifteen-year period starting in 1910. It seems that superintendents, like pastors, often made a circuit from one rescue mission to another. As one of the founders of the Brotherhood of Rescue Mission Superintendents, Mel Trotter related, "Missions were opening so fast, that we were compelled to switch our men around to fit the place."[5] Mel knew that nurturing was the key to successful mission planting.

Robert Allen's first of two identified tenures in Saginaw was said to have been from 1910 to 1917,

when the first world war was raging.[6] This period
however, is rather puzzling in that there are
accounts of three other superintendents, namely,
William Kellogg, Sidney Catherman and George
Dibble serving at different times successively within
the same span.[7] The records fail to resolve the
confusion. Thus far, we can only speculate that
perhaps some extenuating circumstances
interrupted Allen's service.

———————— • ————————

In the spring of 1908, an energetic teenager
named Fred Davis was working as both a bellboy
and secretary to Farnham Lyon, the owner of the
Bancroft Hotel, directly across the street from the
Rescue Mission. Through the witness of a fellow
employee, an elevator operator, Fred came to
know Christ. Soon he began attending, then
taking part in services at the Mission, and on the
street. One night Superintendent George Trotter
told him that he was to deliver three sermons from
the Gospel Wagon. The first was to be in South
Saginaw. "In my mind I framed the talk," recalled
Fred in a 1932 interview with the Saginaw Daily
News:

Had I been able to say what I had planned,
the sermon probably would have rivaled
Lincoln's Gettysburg address for its profound
influence on the Christian world.

When I got on my feet, however, something told me that the crowd was anything but friendly. I mumbled something or other and sat down. To this day, I haven't the slightest idea what I said.[8]

That humble beginning apparently did not discourage Fred. Instead, it turned out to be an important step in proving his mettle in the Lord's work. A few years later, George Dibble, who was Mission Superintendent in 1912, hired Fred as Assistant Superintendent.

George & Lura Ellen Dibble
Archives of the Billy Graham Center,
Wheaton, IL - Melvin Ernest
Trotter Collection

Rev. Fred Davis

Later the Board called him as Superintendent. At that time, 1917, he was heading the insurance division of the Flint Vehicle Factory Mutual Benefit Association and Vehicle Club. "I had to choose between a job that meant several thousands of dollars a year to me in the business world and one that would pay me $100 a

month," Davis said. The urge to return to
Christian service won out. This is just one
example among scores of Mission staffers with
qualifications that enabled them to pursue more
profitable careers. Instead they chose sacrifice in
order to serve the homeless and needy for the
glory of God and His Kingdom. Fred subsequently
answered the call of God into pastoral ministry. In
separate tenures he served as pastor of the First
Baptist and Fordney Avenue Baptist Churches in
Saginaw, and the Broadway Baptist Church, Bay
City. Even so, Rev. Davis' scope of activities was
not bound by denomination and made him a
significant figure in Saginaw's civic development.[9]

——————— • ———————

Before finding Christ in 1908, Vance Shober,
who was Superintendent in 1918, had lived as a
hobo for seventeen years. As part of his testimony
he coined the title, "Shober—saved, shaved and
sober."[10]

The peace that followed World War I would
soon see a culmination of the long active
temperance movement that Billy Sunday, R.A.
Torrey and others had a hand in. Hence
prohibition, the banning of alcoholic beverages,
became the law of the land under the 18th
amendment to the U.S. Constitution. The

immediate backlash however, was rampant defiance of the law.[11] Along with it, moral restraints were cast aside, ushering in the *roaring twenties* and changing society's mores as a result.

Following a three-year pastorate of the South Park Baptist Church in Port Huron, Rev. Robert Allen returned in the fall of 1921 to resume directing the Saginaw Mission.[12]

———————•———————

In 1923, Rev. Bob Ingersoll took over management of the Rescue Mission.[13] Given up as hopeless by both the courts and loved ones, he was jailed in Grand Rapids when Mel Trotter paid him a visit and led him to Christ.[14] Bob went on to assist Mel in overseeing the Pacific Garden Mission after Harry Monroe passed away.[15] He then became Superintendent there from 1915 – 1918 and was an evangelist of eminent renown.

The Ingersoll daughters, Loraine Birdsall and Barbara Morgan, together with their respective husbands, William and Edward, were well identified with the Saginaw Rescue Mission, in particular, the ministry of music. A pianist and organist, both of which he taught, Bill Birdsall met Jesus at the Mission just three months before Rev. Ingersoll became Superintendent.[16] His romance with Loraine began as he accompanied her singing for a Mission service. She regularly did vocal solo as well as ensemble work with her sister and others at Mission functions. Ed Morgan would serve as song leader. Bill also served as Business Manager and Assistant Superintendent of the Mission during the 1960s, as well as Vice President of the Board of Directors.[17]

———————•———————

Among the earliest converts of the Saginaw Rescue Mission was an inebriate drifter by the name of Jim Daubney. Back in his hometown of Oldham, England, he began learning the trade of cabinetmaking at age 14. After taking up boxing, he found he was able to earn a living as a prize fighter. At a *spirited* farewell party for friends departing for railroad work in Nova Scotia, Jim was pulled aboard a train. The next thing he remembered was waking up on a vessel well on its way across the North Atlantic. No matter. He had no fetters to restrain his wanderlust for adventure. Besides, the "accidental" immigrant had always wanted to see America. The shackles of enslavement to alcohol however, were slowly tightening their throttling grip.

As providence would have it, it was no fluke that Jim should ultimately land in Saginaw; neither was his passage in front of the Mission in 1906. Upon leaving a Genesee Avenue saloon in search of yet merrier liquid refreshment, he was drawn several doors west by the sound of hearty, worshipful singing coming from the 'old lighthouse.' Little did he realize in that moment that his pathway would lead him through the Door to new Life.

Superintendent George Trotter preached on the person and work of Christ. Jim had never heard anything like it in his life. Irresistibly, he listened to compelling testimonies of fellow young men whose lives were made over by a personal encounter with God. Without hesitation, he decided he wanted this Jesus. At the same time, he noted all desire for alcohol left him, permanently.[18] Like so many formerly deceived by a counterfeit version of joy, Jim in turn would begin seeking others to rescue from ruin. He soon was able to obtain a day job in a local factory. Every night was spent in Mission services or Bible classes. Four years later he embarked on a career in rescue mission ministry. He began in Detroit, then Milwaukee, Sioux Falls, South Dakota, and Rock Island, Illinois.

True to custom, in the spring of 1926 the Mission scheduled a special series of evangelistic meetings. The guest preacher would be the Superintendent of the City Rescue Mission of Springfield, Massachusetts, James Daubney. A few months later he would return from New England, answering a call to take charge of the ministry through which he was born again.[19]

WAS A PRIZE FIGHTER—NOW A CHURCH MEMBER.

JAMES DAUBNEY

WHAT a difference in the morning. Sept. 3rd, 1906, I was passing the *Mission* a stranger and no place to go, I heard the singing and went inside and heard the boys tell what Jesus had done for them, and I said if there is anything in this life of serving Jesus Christ I am going to try it, as it costs nothing. and I did accept Christ as my Savior and *I'll tell you, friends, it has been the happiest days of my life. When I struck the Mission*, friends, I was just as far down in sin through drink as it was possible for a man to be.

I thought that I hadn't a friend in the world but my dear old mother and father who are thousands of miles away. But how soon I was to find out that Jesus loved me. Since that night I have never had any desire for the old things that were sending me down to hell. Think, friends, what it means for me to be leading a Christian life; a man that led an awful life for 10 years, doing no work; just traveling the country; there was no limit to the money I used to get, but since accepting Christ I have been happier without a cent in my pockets. I used to think that it was impossible for a man to enjoy himself if he was not in a saloon drinking whiskey or smoking cigars, but friends, those good times are not on the map with the good times the Christian people have. I tell you this is not fiction. Just you try it. You will never regret it; for if ever a man has seen both sides of life, it is me, and I thank God for saving me and giving me such peace, joy and happiness, and it is my only desire to live to obey this blessed Savior.

Chapter 11
Increasing Vigil Through The Long Dark Night

Recognizing a need to serve growing numbers of transient as well as elderly men, Daubney's leadership brought an expansion of both the Mission's services and identity. New strides were made in cooperating with other benevolent agencies of the community, particularly as the Mission in 1928 became a member of the Welfare League (later identified as the Community Chest and today known as the United Way).[1] The aim was to make the Mission a kind of clearinghouse in concert with recognition as an emergency shelter. Hence eleven new beds were installed along with shower facilities and first-aid equipment. Local children were provided free baths on Saturdays—boys in the morning and girls in the afternoon.

Properly accommodating the needy could be a labor-intensive task for Mission staff. Homeless transients typically arrived in such an unkempt condition that they required delousing.[2] Thus fumigating equipment was acquired. Despite any past negative stereotype of rescue missions in the public mind, it should be fully understood that, as an agency devoted to relief, the Saginaw Rescue Mission has always maintained safety and cleanliness as essential priorities, especially accompanying its spiritual emphasis.* Furthermore, as an emergency lodging and food service facility, the Mission simply wouldn't be able to meet health codes and remain open without a dedication to high standards. Through the years the Mission kitchen has maintained good to perfect ratings by Health Department inspectors.

------

*"Cleanliness is next to godliness," rose to prominence as a national motto for cleaning up America's cities in the late nineteenth and early twentieth centuries. This was due to the fact that rapidly multiplying populations were creating overwhelmingly daunting sanitation problems and breeding grounds for disease as a result. Those were days of the old slum missions, particularly in larger cities. Some of these did have flophouses that were little more than holdouts for the wrecking ball. As such, they were rather unsanitary, however, those conditions are long since gone thanks to the development of stringent sanitary laws.[3]

The move back to the Weadock corner took place in the late spring of 1927. In a little over two years however, the facility would begin to prove woefully inadequate for serving the needy whose numbers would soon take a quantum leap virtually off the chart.

All at once, the stock market crashed on October 29, 1929. America's economy began to collapse as a result, so initiating the Great Depression. The cataclysmic reversal of fortune crushed the nation's spirit, yet its effects were suffered worldwide. Foreclosures forced innumerable families out of their homes and into the streets. Many packed it in for new frontiers.

Besides shelter, the foremost pursuit was finding morsels of food enough to make it through just one more day. Thousands died of disease resulting from malnutrition.[4] Resources were conserved and stretched in creative ways not conceived of before. The concepts of 'all-for-one' and 'team player' took on new meaning. Even the youngest children were expected to use whatever capability they had to help eke out the family's survival.

Multitudes of homeless families gave rise to *squatter settlements* across the country. *Phoenixville,* was named for Saginaw Mayor George Phoenix, who had promoted the community's development. The crude array of shacks stretched north of the Center Street Bridge along the Saginaw River. By 1937, the City Council, fearful of a deadly disaster—should the makeshift encampment wash away in spring floods—shut it down.[5]

The Depression era served to both temper and ennoble an entire generation. Even so, many a spirit broke under the pressure of hard times, scuttling ambition and swelling the ranks of the drifter in myriad numbers. In desperate search of brighter horizons, men stole aboard boxcars, riding the rails from one town to the next.[6] Lamentably, so did thousands of young people. The illicit practice itself was inherently dangerous, especially when a train was on the move; so was the lifestyle as it was often the way of outlaws.

Ragged transients found clothing even harder to come by than food because missions gave most of their garments to needy local residents. In those days most people couldn't afford to let their old clothes go so they made do for as long as they possibly could. For this reason, stocks of donated items at the Saginaw Rescue Mission would dwindle, but also because they were often given out as fast as they came in. Consequently, through a necessitated screening process, only those deemed deserving of articles received them, however, as much was given to those who didn't ask, as to those who did.[7]

Preparing shoes for free distribution to the needy.

Saginaw was no exception to communities across the nation that saw the advent of *hobo jungles*.* Similar to squatter settlements, homeless

---

*Actually, the term *hobo* originated as "Ho, beau!"—a greeting between migratory workers. As such, hoboes had a reputation for pitching in to earn a meal, proudly distinguishing themselves from *bums* or people who refused to work.[10]

transients inhabited these camps, usually situated near train yards. One stood amidst a wooded area near the Saginaw River bank, northwest of the Johnson Street Bridge. Another was in the nearby Davenport dump region. When inclement weather set in, a phrase coined among the men was, *three hots and a cot*, preferring shelter at the Rescue Mission over kindling an evening fire in "Pussyville"[8] (no doubt named for the abundance of pussy willows). Regrettably, beds were often only available for roughly one third of those seeking them. For example, a report for just the month of March 1930 stated that 1,283 men had slept on the floor compared to 496 who were fortunate enough to enjoy the comfort of a clean bed.[9]

Overburdened operations languished at Lapeer and Weadock through the first three years of the Depression. During the period, appeals were made to the public for larger facilities to ease overcrowding. Nearly 7,000 men, young and old, slept on the floor in 1931. About ten times a month, it was necessary to stack beds so that the dormitories could be set up for meal service to the overflow of hungry people. Each day an average of 230 men, women and children were using a single rest room with one toilet.[11] Relief finally arrived in late November 1932 when the final move on Lapeer took place (three blocks east).

December 4, 1937 at 921 Lapeer Avenue. The hungry await the serving of a satisfying meal.

Formerly owned by the late George Spring, two conjoined buildings at the corner of Lapeer and Third were purchased from Frankenmuth State Bank. The compound address was 521-27 (reflecting four previous business sites) but the number would later change simply to 921. In its own home for the first time, the building considerably expanded available space for ministry operations at a time when it was most urgently needed. Several large rooms were allocated for the warehousing of donated goods, from clothing and shoes, to furniture, heating equipment and other household items. The purchase seemed providential too, in that it was made without increasing overhead or adding to the overall budget.[12] Thus the Mission remained and developed from this site over the next fifty years.

In exchange for the care received, there was plenty of work to do at the Mission. Loafing was not an option. Not only was there constant cleaning, but maintaining the facility included repairing, plastering, painting and assisting with renovations. Grateful clients proved invaluable in these capacities. The addition of the basement at Lapeer and Third was one example. Both the digging and dirt removal were done by hand. Clients also performed most of the construction of the two-story expansion completed in 1935.[13] By this time, a daily average of 200 people eating at the Mission were better served by the new addition.[14]

James Daubney

Mr. Daubney's leadership advanced the efforts of the Mission's employment bureau. Jobs were found for both men and women. While most jobs for men were temporary, some developed into steady positions. Permanent employment was more readily available for women than for men.

Meetings continued on the street as well as in the factories, jail, hospitals, and the County Home. Bible classes were attended by an average of 60 men, three times a week. Sunday School attendance reached 300, necessitating a temporary move to First Congregational Church. Youngsters taking part in the choir alone numbered 60. A Bible class for teens was created.[15] The Mission also had its own Cub Scout, Boy Scout and Girl Scout troops. The weekly women's and baby clinic, conducted by Dr. Esther L. Eymer was said to have the largest attendance of any such clinic in the city.

Boys and girls of the Mission's Sunday School, 1934. Standing far left - Mission Superintendent James Daubney. Second row far left - Sydney Dunkerley. Far right standing - Mrs. James (Florence) Daubney.

Sunday School children prepare to depart for a trip to the Detroit Zoo.

Handicraft time in the Mission's Sunday School. Right - Sydney Dunkerley, boys teacher.

Succeeding her husband in 1938, Florence Daubney was the first and only woman to fill the office of Superintendent in the Saginaw Rescue Mission's first century. James A. "John" Graham was her Assistant.[16]

During her first year, a branch work known as the First Ward Mission was established. Taking over the former Sarah E. Tanner Mission at 1315 North Eighth, this division was expressly devoted to serving homeless African Americans. The facility was a "clean, modern

John Graham

building" maintained by the Rescue Mission under the direct supervision of Mrs. Marie Perttle. Each day, hot meals were prepared at the Rescue Mission, then "rushed to the First Ward Mission in specially constructed trucks." This style of meal service was dubbed the *rolling kitchen*.[17]

Although not definitively stated in the discovered data, one *might* assume, given the times, that the existence of this branch represented racial segregation. However intolerable the idea may be, especially by today's standards, it is important to bear in mind that segregation in those days was status quo throughout American society. Despite that, by no means did either

prejudice or discrimination have a part in the ministry's motive. On the contrary, the intent and focus was that of *inclusiveness* in extending the compassion of Christ to *all* the needy. Therefore, this facet of the ministry was conducted and viewed with pride—even as the Saginaw News related it with no

Florence Daubney

discernible bat of an eye. This in no way is an attempt to justify the practice of keeping races separate, even in retrospect, but rather to frankly relate history as it was, apparently for a period of several years.

Additionally, Friendly House, a fourteen-room home for pensioned senior men of low income, was established at the Lapeer and Third site in the fall of that same year.[18]

John Graham succeeded Mrs. Daubney as Superintendent in 1941. Indications of the First

Ward Mission continuing beyond the next year have not been found. There is, however, evidence of integration at Lapeer and Third beginning quite soon after.[19]

921 Lapeer at Third, circa 1947. Friendly House, Home for Aged Men occupied the brick building at right.

Chapter 12
Changing Times

Rev. Thomas J. Hinkin came as Superintendent in June of 1942. Susie, his wife was at his side overseeing all the women's and children's activities as well as planning meals. He soon selected evangelist John Erskine of Evart, Michigan as Assistant Superintendent. Miss Jessie Fellows was the Home Missionary and Social Welfare Case Worker.[1]

A native of South Wales in Great Britain, Hinkin moved to the United States with his family as a teen in 1895. A skilled bass singer, he was associated with Mel Trotter as a member of the American Four Quartet. He devoted his life to rescue mission ministry after a friend with a drinking problem

asked T. J. to find him a place to stay. As a seasoned
leader in rescue ministry, he was a veteran of missions
in Muskegon, Michigan, Lincoln, Nebraska, and
Cedar Rapids, Iowa before coming to Saginaw.[2]

America's entrance into World War II saw the
end of the Great Depression. Rampant homelessness
likewise, pretty much went away. As millions of
men were called into military service and new jobs
opened as a result, a sharp drop occurred in the
number of transients roaming about.[3] This fact
was mirrored in clearly reduced numbers seeking
shelter at the Rescue Mission.

In the six-month period preceding the Japanese
Empire's attack on Pearl Harbor, 2,007 men
showed up at the Rescue Mission. During the
same period the following year (1942), only 646,
less than a third of the previous year's number,
appeared at the Mission door.[4]

More jobs opened than men to fill them. Hence
"Rosie the Riveter" became the symbol of a swelling
industrial work force of women nationwide.

Following the war, the number of people
seeking Mission services very slowly began to rise
again. By 1949, the drifter was making a
comeback. Compared to his Depression era

counterpart, he was generally about five years older, or middle-aged. Rev. Hinkin had him figured as, "Too old for the factories, too young for an old age pension."[5] A tenderhearted man, Hinkin shunned the commonly coined, insensitive labels for such men. Instead, he preferred the accepted term in rescue mission circles, *transient*.

Tom Hinkin

At any rate, by this time the middle-aged transient man riding the rails was the stereotypical mission lodger. The conception while not inaccurate, may have been overly simplistic. In the not too distant future however, the true profiles of typical rescue mission clients would begin to undergo considerable changes.

The post-war era would also see Child Evangelism Fellowship classes and Vacation Bible School added to the Mission's line-up of services. While the Mission did not offer on-site lodging for women and children, they did at least by

Mrs. Thomas Hinkin

this time have an arrangement with the YWCA for that purpose.[6]

Support is Further Organized

In October 1951, the Women's Auxiliary was formally inaugurated with a charter membership of 54. Formed as a separate organization from the Women's Sewing Circle, the Auxiliary created fellowship between denominations and promoted the work of the Mission among the various churches. Additionally, it began conducting special projects, free-will offerings and drives for obtaining needed equipment at the Mission. Initially, eleven denominations were represented but the number would grow substantially. Mrs. Walter Pierce, wife of the Muskegon Rescue Mission Superintendent at that time, is credited with organizing the group.[7] At its second meeting, officers were elected. Mrs. Harold M. Karls was first president.[8]

Mrs. Walter Pierce (center), Muskegon Rescue Mission, organizer of the Saginaw Rescue Mission Women's Auxillary, discusses plans with Susie Hinkin (right) and Mrs. John Belkema, Muskegon.

Today's Auxiliary operates a lovely Gift Shoppe
which is regularly open to the public at the
Mission. It features a varied array of fine items,
many of them skillfully crafted by hand. Proceeds
of this endeavor likewise benefit the Mission.

Late in 1952, the Mission tallied figures from the
records of its forty-seven year history. A half
million articles of clothing had been given away.
The number of meals served was 1,309,000.
People attending Mission worship services
numbered 400,000 and 100,000 had enrolled in
Bible study. The number of decisions to trust
Christ for salvation was recorded as 5,000.[9]

Naturally, statistics
alone are not the
ultimate measure of
success. Nor is a
ministry's validity
necessarily diminished
by numbers perceived
as meager. On the
other hand, they're not
irrelevant when it
comes to Mission
friends knowing what
their investments of
prayers, volunteer

Miss Jessie Fellows, Home Missionary and Social Welfare Case Worker for the Mission sorts clothing for free distribution to the needy.

efforts and finances are accomplishing, provided the human heart is kept in focus.

Rev. Hinkin's tenure of over twelve years in Saginaw was the longest of his career. While still serving, he was stricken with a lingering illness that ultimately took him home to be with the Lord in 1954.[10]

———————— • ————————

Assistant Superintendent William E. Bowman, who began his duties shortly before Rev. Hinkin's passing, was soon named Superintendent.[11] He would remain in the post less than a year however, and be succeeded by Rev. Perry L. Oden, an Alabaman who was previously Assistant Superintendent of the Mobile Rescue Mission.[12]

William Bowman

After Rev. Gerrit Jager, an Illinois native and

another veteran of rescue ministry, became Superintendent in 1957, a Men's Auxiliary was organized and functioned for a number of years. Today, both men and women are invited to participate in one organization

Perry Oden

simply identified as the Rescue
Mission Auxiliary.

The Mission's family of
supporters, including the Women's
Auxiliary, expanded under Rev.
Jager's watch. Rooms were
painted, a new piano, chairs and
banquet tables were purchased as well.[13]

Gerrit Jager

———————•———————

Rev. Don Price had one of the more checkered
pasts among men later rising to mission leadership.
It was 1960 when he answered the call to the
superintendent's post in Saginaw.

Reared with contempt for law and order, Don
experienced more than his share of rejection as a
child. His dad was shot by police during the
commission of a robbery. Following recovery he
was sentenced to five years in the Indiana State
Penitentiary. In the wake of the resulting divorce,
his mother abandoned Don when he was five
years old. From that day forward he was angry at
the world. To make matters worse, the
grandparents he lived with for the next nine years
abused him. At the age of eight, his grandfather
taught him how to drink liquor.

After dad's release from prison, fourteen-year-old Don went to live with him. He was with his father when he tracked down an old enemy. Watching him beat the man into unconsciousness taught Don a lesson in violence.

As a soldier in the Army during World War II, he drank all he could get away with in quest of a good time. Upon returning to civilian life in Indianapolis, he met and married Lydia Lowry.

New acquaintances introduced Don to the underside of obtaining income, by teaching him the tricks of the burglary trade. Along with gambling, success in crime proved unstable, especially when he was caught and shot in

Don Price

the act. After recovering from two bullet wounds to the back, Don was convicted and sentenced to a year at hard labor on the rock pile.

The anger coloring his life now turned to rage. Scrapping with a fellow prison inmate landed him in a six by six foot hole of solitary confinement. The structure in that section permitted inmates to talk to, but not see each other. Regardless of Don's violent objections, a man lodged nearby persisted in reading Scripture aloud and explaining the plan of salvation to him.

Through all his vehement protesting, Don was listening, and affected enough to promise God that he would attend prison chapel services when he got out of solitary. Keeping his word, he again heard the Gospel but steadfastly refused the invitation to trust Christ. He was tough, he told himself—tough enough to do the time—until he thought of his precious wife and children. Then when a blind girl sang, "No One Ever Cared For Me Like Jesus," Don's old heart of stone broke along with his will. Within seconds of her finish he was at the altar, calling upon the Lord and receiving a new heart of flesh. Ezekiel 36:26.

No One Ever Cared For Me Like Jesus

Words & Music by Charles F. Weigle

I would love to tell you what I think of Jesus,
Since I found in Him a friend so strong and true;
I would tell you how He changed my life completely,
He did something that no other friend could do.
No one ever cared for me like Jesus,
There's no other friend so kind as He;
No one else could take the sin and darkness from me.
O, how much He cared for me.

All my life was full of sin when Jesus found me,
All my heart was full of misery and woe;
Jesus placed His strong and loving arms about me,
And He led me in the way I ought to go.
No one ever cared for me like Jesus,
There's no other friend so kind as He;
No one else could take the sin and darkness from me.
O, how much He cared for me.

Ev'ry day He comes to me with new assurance,
More and more I understand His words of love;
But I'll never know just why He came to save me,
Till some day I see His blessed face above.
No one ever cared for me like Jesus,
There's no other friend so kind as He;
No one else could take the sin and darkness from me.
O, how much He cared for me.

©1932 Singspiration Music, a division of Zomba Enterprises, Inc. (ASCAP) (Administered by Brentwood-Benson Music Publishing) All rights reserved. Used by permission.

Don & Lydia Price

From that moment on Don became a vibrant witness of God's transforming power. Serving the Lord with his whole heart, he dedicated his life to ministry. In the process, he claimed the promise of Acts 16:31: "Believe on the Lord Jesus Christ and you shall be saved; you *and* your household."

He led not only his wife and children to saving faith, but his father, grandfather and an uncle as well.[14] Following Bible school training, he served as Assistant, then as Superintendent in charge of the Mel Trotter Branch Mission of Grand Rapids before coming to Saginaw.[15] His leadership was dynamic. The Mission's family of benefactors again grew as Don further developed the banquet as a feature of the annual support-raising event.

————————•————————

Ralph Brooker

Ralph A. Brooker was yet another man out of hope when the light of a rescue mission shined on him in 1954. He was jobless, without purpose and drinking heavily. Ever since trusting Christ as Savior and Lord, he sought out others in similar circumstances to show the way of new life. Rev. Brooker came to Saginaw as Superintendent in the fall of 1966.[16]

Increasing Faith

By 1969, the Board of Directors was observing that the Community Chest's United Fund was not adequately meeting the Rescue Mission's needs. Spearheaded by Mission President Rollin Severance, the Board was persuaded that withdrawing from its thirty-eight year membership in the Chest would free the Mission to avail itself of other funding sources. They believed the spiritual emphasis would be afforded greater liberty as well.

Rollin Severance

The new vision was that of an expanding network of Mission friends. A broader base of support with a potential for limitless growth would primarily be comprised of voluntary gifts from individuals, churches, businesses, civic organizations and grants from foundations.

In a bold step, the Mission embarked on a new era of independence on January 1st, 1970, as official ties to the United Fund came to a mutually harmonious conclusion. In so doing however, a simultaneous declaration of *dependence* on God was made, identifying the ministry as a faith mission.[17] Bumps and challenges along the road notwithstanding, God has honored the confidence placed in Him. Today employees of the various workplaces participating in the United Way have the opportunity to designate gifts and have them channeled to the Rescue Mission.

Rural Route to Regeneration

Saginaw resident, Thomas Cousineau, was already deeply active in the Saginaw Rescue Mission for many years when he assumed duties as Superintendent. The former truck driver had been in the insurance business for a decade at the time of his appointment. He had taught Bible classes, conducted evening services and took part in the Mission's jail ministry. He was also an officer of the Men's Auxiliary for eight years and a member of the Board of Directors.

Tom was instrumental in developing Mission ministries to include a farm on Curtis Road and summer camps for underprivileged children.[18]

Purchased in 1971, the Mission farm provided a rural setting in which men resided and worked while studying the Bible and learning to walk with Christ.

Tom Cousineau

The purpose of the day camp program on the same site was to introduce boys and girls to the Lord Jesus Christ. Youngsters who would normally not be open to the Gospel became receptive as it was blended

with fun activities like pony rides, games, crafts
and special outings.

Chapter 13
Beaming Brighter And Farther

America was celebrating its Bicentennial in 1976 when a young local businessman by the name of Ken Streeter, a Mission supporter and volunteer was also serving as a member of the Board of Directors. Immediately succeeding Tom Cousineau, he became the twenty-third Superintendent of the Saginaw Rescue Mission and the second Board member in a row to rise to the post. Before long the title would change to Executive Director. Ken's tenure at the helm, well over one fourth of the Mission's history, has by far been the longest. Sometimes those who hold a position for an extensive period of years lapse into mediocrity, merely marking time until retirement. On the contrary, Ken was excited when he started and has increasingly fanned the flames in leading the Rescue Mission through its most dramatic era of development—as a labor of love, and with a sparkling eye on the next century of service. That vision has continually kept a focus on developing more effective ways to help needy people become productive, self-supporting citizens, thereby enabling them to leave homelessness behind.

Under Ken's management, the men's residential Discipleship Program has made strident advances. His approach to mission ministry has been one of sharing leadership opportunities. Ken Bartholomew's directive role was important, as was Lowell Conrad's on the Mission farm. The men especially identified with Rev. Ron Morris, as one who knew firsthand the desperation of addiction but rose to walk in Christ's victory. Rev. Phil MacGown faithfully poured his heart into discipling the men. Darryl Bartlett, who succeeded him, further developed the structure and effectiveness of the Program before accepting a call to head the Holland Rescue Mission (Michigan). Joining the family legacy of dedicated Mission service, Dan Streeter then stepped aboard as Men's Director in 1992 and today is Director of Mission Operations.

It's Been A Great Blessing

The events that led to Ken Arnold's new birth in Christ began early in 1980 when he was

Ken & Joy Arnold

"in the process of self-annihilation. He had lost wife and family. All earthly possessions were taken away, and his source of employment was also gone," related Ken Streeter to

Mission friends. Thus he began a six-month binge of drunkenness. "Day after day of intoxication created a snowball effect, catapulting him toward eventual destruction that he was able to foresee, but not alter.

Nobody can sing the hymn, *Jesus Paid It All* with greater conviction than Ken Arnold, because he met the Lord in the darkest hour of his life. Local police in Ohio would find him behind the steering wheel of his car, fast asleep in the middle of the road. Eventually authorities directed Ken to Akron's Haven of Rest Rescue Mission." This is where he learned about Jesus and trusted Him for salvation.

Former Saginaw Rescue Mission Chaplain, Ron Morris, was especially close to Ken, because both men met Christ through the Akron Mission. Ken continued learning to walk in fellowship with the Lord at the Saginaw Rescue Mission. He studied God's Word in greater depth at Elohim Bible Institute in Castile, New York, and has worked for missions in Florida and Washington State as well as Saginaw where he settled.

Since meeting Christ, Ken has discovered *joy* in more ways than one. Joy happens to be the woman he met at church and married in 1986. "I just praise Him every day," says Ken of living for Jesus. "I have a home, a great wife, everything I need. If He wasn't there, the power of prayer and all the supportive people, I wouldn't be here today. It's been a great blessing. Compared to smoking, drinking, cussing and running around, I've had more fun with Christian people than I thought possible."

———————— • ————————

As part of their commitment to the Program, clients live at the Mission for up to a year. Through daily Bible study and cultivation of a personal relationship with Christ, they learn to walk in victory over chemical dependency and other life controlling problems. It's called *Life With*

A Purpose and applicants must pass a thirty-day qualifying process to gain formal enrollment. Personal discipline is developed through four stages of advancement. In the process, the individual is equipped with practical life skills for independent living beyond the Mission. Each level entrusts the client with increased privileges and responsibilities, culminating in graduation. A vital component to the success of the Program is the relationship each client develops with a chosen mentor. One on one, they meet together for counseling, prayer, reviewing of goals and addressing challenges.

Christ His First Love Now

Eddie Rice

As a young man, I came home from Viet Nam very troubled, not really knowing any direction, so I turned to the world. I was married twice, neither marriage working out. My second wife and I left Saginaw because I had gotten laid off from Wickes Corporation. And we went to Alabama where we stayed for seven years. We had one daughter, and to make a long story short, my wife got pregnant by my best friend. I brought her back to Saginaw to be near her family, and then I started drinking and hanging with the wrong crowd. It was during this time that I was introduced to drugs, and my life really began falling apart. When I hit rock bottom I lost everything that I had. I had nowhere to stay. It was then that I remembered the Saginaw Rescue Mission. When I was a child they would always give my aunt food for us. There were five of us and we were poor.

When I came to the Mission I met a true man of God named Darryl Bartlett. Mr. Bartlett was a good Bible teacher who regularly taught us to put Jesus first in our lives, and that everything else would fall into place. He taught us to be obedient to God and live a disciplined life. That's where I began to find God. Even though He was there all the time, I didn't know it. He had already chosen me to be one of His children. It was at this time that I also met Ken Streeter. He was a great man of God and you could see Him working in his life. Ken became my mentor and a true friend.

It was then that the enemy saw my weakness. I went through some storms, trials, and tribulations. I lost my first love for God, but He never turned from me. Every time I fell down, He would pick

me up. Friends and family wrote me off, but I
prayed to God in Heaven. It took awhile to learn
that I had to obey Him (Acts 5:29). He put two
men in my life at the Saginaw Rescue Mission to
make a nothing into a something. People wrote
me off, but God wrote me in. Now I am saved,
baptized, confessing that Jesus is the Son of the
Living God, and I have repented of my sins. I
have become a slave to God. It is no longer I who
live in this fleshly body, it is Christ, and His Holy
Spirit lives within me. He is in control of my life.
It is no longer my will, but His will that guides
me. I love God over everything in this world.

The Liberation of Literacy

As the Program itself developed, Mission staff
observed that many of the men lacked adequate
educational skills to make them candidates for
good jobs. Hence in 1990, three volunteers
stepped forward to begin teaching classes that
would prepare clients for attaining the General
Education Development certificate (GED), the
equivalent of a high school diploma. This new
aspect of the Discipleship Program was the
forerunner of today's Literacy Education Center at
the Mission. The faculty comprised of Vicki

Apperson, Norm Kanouse and Sue Schell team-
taught the classes three times each week. Their
outstanding service won recognition from outside
the Mission auspices when they were honored
with the J.C. Penney Golden Rule Award. The

**Vicki Apperson, Norm Kanouse and Sue Schell with the J.C.
Penney Golden Rule Award.**

added objective of completing high school also
served to solidify the men's goal of graduating
from the Program.

Workplace requirements increasingly call for
some computer knowledge and experience. The
Mission's educational program began with one
computer. Through donations there would soon
be five that were utilized for a number of years.
Software programs enable clients to tutor
themselves in math, information skills, writing,
language arts, and reading.

From Hopeless Addict to Child of God

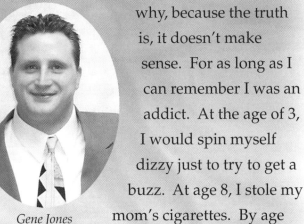

Gene Jones

Everybody wants to figure out why they're addicted. Well I stopped trying to figure out why, because the truth is, it doesn't make sense. For as long as I can remember I was an addict. At the age of 3, I would spin myself dizzy just to try to get a buzz. At age 8, I stole my mom's cigarettes. By age 12, I started sniffing glue and paint. Then when I was 15, I drank a bottle and a half of rubbing alcohol. That put me in the hospital—I almost died. Doctors thought I was attention-hungry or suicidal but I just wanted to get drunk. At seventeen I left home. That's when I started doing other drugs—weed and crack cocaine. I was very rebellious—thought I was smarter than everybody. After a year I checked into a treatment center. That was the first time I had ever considered that I might be an alcoholic, but I denied it. I continued to deny it when I went back to Alcoholics Anonymous to please my fiancée, but she left anyway. A.A. teaches that you must believe in a power greater than yourself. That's where I found myself up against a wall. I thought *'what power?'*—I just didn't get it. By age 25 I was drinking three fifths of gin a day.

At 27 I was arrested for D.U.I. (driving under the influence). After 60 days I was allowed to go to work for a temp agency and moved to Avenue B in Flint. I didn't know it but it was probably the worst 'crack' street in Flint. So my sister in Saginaw invited me to come live with her. I got a job at Sears but after two months I began drinking again. I then moved to a motel nearby, but I would get so drunk that I'd sleep through my shift. Alcohol attaches to the nervous system, purging endorphins. You then get what's called a "wet brain," so when I'd stop drinking, my nerves were just shot. I would have delirium and hallucinations. It got to the point where I just couldn't work anymore. I had $3-4,000 in savings so I lived off that until it ran out. I got so sick I could barely walk.

I then began going to outpatient counseling. By September 18, 2003, I realized I was hopeless—I had had so much love in me and willingness to help people but alcohol destroyed it—and I began dying. I felt my organs shutting down. The only problem was I was afraid to go to hell.

The next day when I woke up I knew I had to move out and go to the detox unit at Healthsource. To stave off the delirium shakes, I bought two 40 ounce bottles of malt liquor, but it didn't work." That would be the last drop of drink Gene would ever take. "When the guy came from detox, he could see how sick I was." Three days in the Pathways unit were followed by eighteen days at DOT Caring Center. Gene was now clean and sober, but still hopeless and frustrated.

With nowhere to go, he turned to the Rescue Mission. "When you're homeless, that's where you go," he related. "I figured I owed it to the people who helped me to try my hardest, even though I was hopeless. My second night at the Mission, I heard the Gospel for the first time. I went forward in response to the invitation but still didn't believe. When I went to bed, full of anxiety and fear, I talked to God: 'I don't know if I believe, but I need You to take this hopelessness and anxiety.'

The next day when I was told about the Discipleship Program, I didn't know if I wanted it. I still didn't believe in salvation. I have the type of mind that wants to understand everything. But Greg Francis said, "Let's get started with the paper work." When I entered the Program I hated it. It was intensive. It wasn't natural living with twenty other men. I was still arrogant, but I was grateful for a warm place to sleep. In A.A. I remember someone saying, 'Try praying to God to help you so you can help others.' God used my hopelessness to break me so that I would surrender and dedicate my life to serving Him."

Part of the Program for Gene was joining "Reformers Unanimous." David Koffman, council leader with the group bought a Bible, which he had specially personalized for Gene. Seeing his name imprinted on the same cover with 'Holy Bible' deeply affected him.

"Life today is awesome," declares Gene. "I've been transformed through God's Word." A church member and salesman with a local furniture outlet, Gene is also a council leader and steward of three Reformers Unanimous transitional houses. "I'm still praying, but I think I would like to go to seminary and preach—possibly pastor—but if overseeing these houses is what God wants me to do, that's fine."

Chapter 14
The New Face
of Homelessness

As the 1980s got underway, America was beginning to experience a new period of sustained economic growth and prosperity. Oddly, at the same time, an old dilemma was once again rearing its ugly head. Homelessness was resurging in numbers not seen since the Great Depression, but with different characteristics. Seemingly with a vengeance, it would dig its heels in and not let go. Although the supply of low-income housing was tightening,[1] this time there was not a collapsing economy to blame. Research shows that most homeless people suffer from mental illness, alcoholism and drug abuse.[2]

Further study revealed a direct link to fractured
family relationships.[3]

Prior to the 1960s, our society was still enjoying
a moral climate established by Biblical tradition. It
wasn't all adding up however, for young people
being reared with permissive new parenting
practices—and they began to observe a manifest
hypocrisy in the older generation. Even as marital
fidelity slid and the divorce rate rose,[4] parents
insisted, "Do as I say, not as I do." Angry and
embittered, the younger generation rebelled.
Throwing out the proverbial baby with the bath
water, the so-called *new morality* of the 1960s
introduced the idea of casual sex and cohabitation
outside the bonds of holy matrimony—*as socially
acceptable*. With bad seed sown and cultivated,
generation next suffered the fallout—a harvest of
decaying family integrity.

Of the Bible Abraham Lincoln said, "This book . . .
is the best gift God has given to man . . . But for it
we could not know right from wrong." If not a
root cause, the banning of prayer and Bible
reading in the public schools, at the very least,
didn't help matters as America cast off its moral
moorings. What solid basis then is left for
knowing what right and wrong *are,* let alone the

difference. "If the foundations be destroyed, what can the righteous do?" Psalm 11:3.

Since the modern era was also a time when commitment laws changed, a considerable portion of those facing life on the streets were people released from mental institutions. But the full picture was yet to come into focus.

For a number of years Ken and the Board had considered a responsibility before God to make the gamut of Mission ministries available to *all* sectors of the needy and homeless of Mid-Michigan. There was no question that the time had come to expand facilities to dimensions that would call for the first Mission relocation in half a century.

Once an upscale apartment house built in the 1920s, the former Eventide Home for seniors operated by the Salvation Army became available.

As the move was considered, the Mission's rural programs on Curtis Road were re-evaluated. Sadly, the conviction that emerged was that these programs had not been cost-effective. Consequently, the Mission farm was closed and the clients from that program joined the other men downtown.

Situated some six blocks east of Lapeer and Third, $125,000 would be needed to purchase the 30,000 square foot Eventide building. Remodeling and equipment purchases would require an additional $75,000. Mission friends enthusiastically responded to the challenge, the move was made to the northwest corner of Burt Street and East Genesee, and the facility was dedicated on June 5th, 1982.

Today's Saginaw Rescue Mission, 1021 Burt at E. Genesee.

Ample space for ministry development was now in hand, just in time to accommodate a homeless population that was not only increasing but also diversifying.

While Mid-Michigan may not have the larger concentrations of long-term homeless like the

more populous metropolitan areas, there is no
question that the plight is more acute than it has
been in many decades, particularly across gender
and generational lines alike. Hurting families
appear at an unprecedented level and are being
displaced as a result. On the other hand, it comes
as no surprise that families with strong marital
bonds, for the most part, are not found among
the homeless.

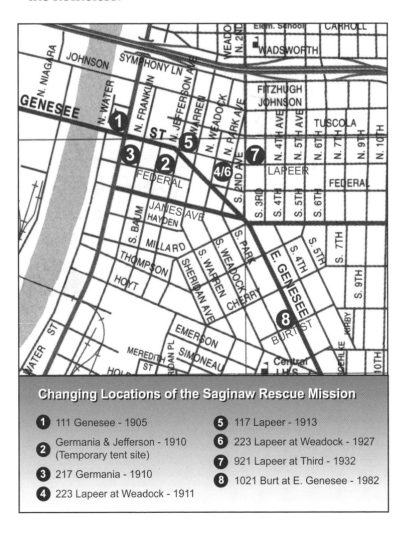

Changing Locations of the Saginaw Rescue Mission

1 111 Genesee - 1905

2 Germania & Jefferson - 1910 (Temporary tent site)

3 217 Germania - 1910

4 223 Lapeer at Weadock - 1911

5 117 Lapeer - 1913

6 223 Lapeer at Weadock - 1927

7 921 Lapeer at Third - 1932

8 1021 Burt at E. Genesee - 1982

Who has suffered the most from society's long
moral decline? The modern typical homeless
person revealed a tragic new face. In an age when
greater numbers of women are pursuing
successful careers and earning more money than
ever before, *children,* accompanied by their
mothers as sole supporters, were now surpassing
the ranks of transient males.[5]

**Another Door Opens . . . *"for of such is the
kingdom of heaven."****

The plaintive cries of mother and child could no
longer go unanswered. Hence on January 1st, 1983,
the Rescue Mission opened the Family Shelter on
the new Burt Street facility's third floor. Safe,
clean, emergency lodging with a loving Christian
witness was now available to homeless women
and children. It was one of the first ministries of
this distinction among missions nationwide.

---

*Mark 10:14.

Robin Tyndall and Karen Streeter initiated the work. On average, five clients a night were served during the first year.

The early days were not without discouragement. A financial crisis in 1984 forced the Family Shelter to temporarily close doors for a period of eight months. Thankfully, Mission friends rallied to the cause through a campaign called *Second Mile Sunday* in the churches, and a program called *Day of Love*. Voluntary gifts underwriting days of Family Shelter operation were accrued.

Ken & Karen Streeter

As days of sponsorship multiplied, the fledgling ministry prepared to open once again.

Little did we realize what the future held in store as the need for the Family Shelter would intensify.

The traditional stereotype of rescue mission clientele thus is history. If the intractability of contemporary homelessness isn't dreadful enough, add the ranks of women and children that would keep mounting more than any other sector of the homeless population year by year. Consistently, this fact has been mirrored in those seeking Mission services locally. We continue to serve a significant number of usually younger transient men, but the majority of Saginaw Rescue Mission clients today are women and children. They hail from the local area for the most part and indicate that they plan to remain in the region.[6]

"Homelessness is primarily a family issue that must be dealt with locally," explained Mission Director Ken Streeter. "The underlying major cause of homelessness today is the breakdown of the family. Our experience shows that the alarming rate of homelessness will not decrease until we address the issues of restoring family relationships."

Miracle of Restoration

When a child is sick, a mother frets. So it was for Roberta Jones when one of her seven children had to be taken to the Emergency room. Compounding the problem was the fact that this family was homeless. A cloud of anxiety would accompany them until mom learned that the child would not need to be admitted. At the hospital, Roberta saw a number to call if you were in need of shelter.

It was October 1986. Roberta and William Jones were in the storm of their lives having just lost their home to foreclosure. As a result, this once happy marriage would crumble in divorce.

The Jones Family

When Roberta phoned the Saginaw Rescue Mission's Family Shelter, she knew right away that she had done the right thing. The compassionate voice on the line gave her a sense of calm and

peace. It was Women's Director, Robin Tyndall.
She encouraged her to come in for an interview.
There was plenty of room. Relieved but hesitant,
reflected Roberta, "I just didn't know what to
expect. It was such a scary time in my life." God
reminded her of Elisha in II Kings 6:15-17. When
Elisha's servant feared the surrounding enemy,
God revealed a far greater company of warriors
protecting them. At that point Roberta took the
first step to restore her family.

"The staff was absolutely wonderful," she
declared. "God did some awesome things while
we were there." She found the order and structure
within the Family Shelter to be very helpful to
both she and her children. William agreed to be
counseled by Mission Director, Ken Streeter, who
made such a positive impact on the family.

Roberta and the children placed a bold faith and
trust in God to provide a new home. "Not a day
went by that we didn't pray for it," she affirmed,
until God directed her to contact a realtor. With no
money and foreclosure on their credit, she didn't
know how but was confident that God would
make a way. Little William Jr. reminded mom that
this was not her battle but the Lord's. He began
praying and thanking God for their new home as
if they already had it. "I was so impressed with

my son's prayers that I began to do the same,"
remarked Roberta. Soon God gave her the
boldness to approach her credit union. She
explained her need of a home and how she and
the children were staying at the Rescue Mission.
Without flinching, the loan officer said, "We'll
have you and your children in a home by
Christmas." True to his word, on December 9,
1986, Roberta and the children moved into their
new home.

William and Roberta's severed marriage was
later restored with all the children taking part in
the ceremony. Since then, four more children were
added to the family. The older children have
successfully pursued college educations and
careers, but Roberta is most proud that her entire
family is serving God. The marriage is stronger
than ever, they are active in their church and are
giving back to the ministry that rescued them. In
Mission chapel services Roberta regularly speaks
and passes on what was so freely given to her—
hope.

Chapter 15

To Rescue A Village

From its inception the Rescue Mission has naturally included senior citizens in its field of compassionate vision. Among the needy, our venerable elders deserve tender loving care as a matter of honor as well as responsibility. Again, the Mission's tradition of care and assistance for disadvantaged seniors demonstrates the reality of God and His perfect love. This of course was the reason Friendly House was established back in the 1930s.

Ever since Saginaw County opened Community Village in 1976, the Rescue Mission regularly referred homeless seniors there when it became evident that their needs of long-term housing and

care required more professional assistance. The
Village was the place of choice because seniors
wholly dependent on Social Security could live
just as comfortably as those able to afford private
payment.

In 1991, God began
to orchestrate a turn of
events that ultimately
led to the Rescue
Mission acquiring
Community Village as
a new division of
ministry. There were
momentous hurdles to
overcome in the
process, however,
God's blessing was
witnessed as the

Mission stepped forward in faith.

First there was excitement, then came
heartbreak.

The Village had been licensed as an infirmary
and Michigan law restricts such operations to
county governments only. Since Saginaw County
was losing a thousand dollars a day in the venture
by this time, it became necessary to sell the facility.

The City Rescue Mission demonstrated a commitment to preserve Community Village's excellent qualities, lauded as unique in Michigan. Therefore, the County Board of Commissioners selected the Mission as the successful bidder to purchase and operate the Village as a home for the aged. To their credit, in accepting the offer, the Board maintained a focus on the needs of less fortunate seniors over the real estate value for the County.

Originally, the Mission offered $375,000 for the purchase. Fulfilling the new designation as a home for the aged however, called for different licensing. Consequently, a number of inspections revealed that complying with 1990s building codes would mandate significant renovations to the facility. Since Saginaw County was not in a position to underwrite the cost of accomplishing the task estimated at two million dollars, the Mission's subsequent offer of $1 for the property "as is" was accepted.

Lamentably, the work required was extensive enough that the Mission had no choice but to close the Village during the project. As a result, 72 residents—especially vulnerable to the stresses of personal upheaval—temporarily lost their home and were forced to seek other accommodations.

"You had to be present to experience the hurt and despair of people who were losing friends, security, quality of life, and perhaps life itself," recalled Mission Director Ken Streeter. "The only salve that could be applied to their wounds was encouragement that the Village would reopen in six months if it was at all possible."

Community Village, 3200 Hospital Road

Photo By Dale Wieck

"We didn't particularly have a desire to grow larger or take on more staff or more responsibility," Ken explained, "but we realized that if there was going to be a home available for senior citizens who depended solely on Social Security benefits for their livelihood, the Rescue Mission was going to need to step up to the challenge of restoring and reopening Community Village."

Happily, as the capital campaign got underway, the company of friends supporting both the

Village and the Rescue Mission expanded once again. Unfortunately, the period of time required to make reopening a reality stretched from six months to seventeen.

It was a triumphant day when state inspectors gave the final go-ahead. Happier still when on May 10th, 1993, the doors officially opened once again to welcome returning and new residents back home. Lingering anticipation was a dream come true at last.

Chapter 16
Preparing the Way Ahead

As the 1990s progressed, Mission staff began recognizing a disturbingly recurring pattern. About ten percent of all clients were returning within a year because they again found themselves homeless. Thankfully, this ratio was found to be quite low compared to national statistics. Yet the repeaters could invariably be identified as drug addicted, high school dropouts, unemployable, and single mothers lacking skills to manage home and children. For these reasons the Mission was compelled to address the need of further equipping clients with enough effective mentoring to overcome their homelessness—permanently.

By 1996, the national rate of homelessness among women and children escalated to 63%.[1] New admissions to the Mission's Family Shelter were paralleling this level with the inevitable result of overcrowding. On many occasions that year the Shelter was forced to supplement its 35 beds with another 15 cots. Increasingly the situation became a regular occurrence. Through the course of 1998, extra cots were set up more nights than any previous year in the Family Shelter.

Long range plans to expand the Family Shelter were already in place but it was now obvious that it was time for development and implementation. The staff and Board of Directors in fact would invest three years in this pursuit with the added foresight of equipping the entire Mission for its next century of service. What emerged was by far the most ambitious and dynamic expansion in the history of the Saginaw Rescue Mission—an addition that would nearly double the size of the Burt Street facility, and establish a Family Empowerment Center.

For openers, the new addition would indeed expand ministries to women and children. Even more importantly, it would offer a residential program similar to the one available to men but be tailored especially for women. Additionally, the project would increase space needed for offices and other existing programs.

Again, Mission friends stepped up to the challenge. *Mission 2000*, a three-year, 3.3 million dollar capital fund drive kicked off in January 1998. The U. S. Department of Housing and Urban Development granted $420,000 to the project. Then when the Andersen Foundation stepped forward with a gift of $500,000, ground was broken in late July. By April 1999, the first and fourth levels of the new addition passed inspections and the Discipleship Program for women commenced.

Family Empowerment Center taking shape, Autumn 1998.

The completed Frank N. Andersen Family Empowerment Center was formally dedicated on October 15, 2000. It features transitional housing

A portion of the Literacy Education Center's computer lab.

for women while they learn to overcome dependency on chemical substances. During their stay (lasting up to one year), they have the opportunity to complete high school through the Literacy Education Center in-house. The new Center boasts a twenty-station computer lab. Job skills and work experience are likewise acquired. Effective parenting skills are taught *and* put into practice because children are able to reside with mom while she builds a new life. This aspect differs from most substance abuse programs that require the family to separate during treatment. Homemaking skills are taught in the F.E.C.'s amply equipped kitchen classroom. The new dining room allows up to 96 women and children to be served. The lovely new Mission Chapel seats 175 and is equipped with a fine sound and video system.

Women's Discipleship Program's First Graduate_____

Learning to Lean on Jesus

When I came to the Mission I had nowhere else to go. I was an alcoholic—a very mean alcoholic, and because everything I tried failed, I thought I would die an alcoholic. But God had other plans for me. When Robin Tyndall told me about the Women's Discipleship Program (which was to begin in about one month), sticking with it for a year sounded kind of hard. But I reasoned: I had spent the better

Cheryl Taylor

part of my life ruining it—what was one year to try to fix it. I had been in other programs for drinking but this one was unique. This one focused on life in the present and the hereafter. I fixed my eyes on God and He took that taste for alcohol and cigarettes away physically and mentally. No cravings, just like a new born person for real. From then on it was a new way of thinking and living.

It hasn't been perfect over the last five years. I lost my dear friend, my son-in-law, and my loving mother. But I have learned to lean on Jesus. I was blessed with a granddaughter and a job in 2000 and I enjoy both of them now, especially my Jadin. I could use some more workdays but I don't let that worry me because I know the Lord didn't bring me all this way to leave me. Whether good or bad I turn to my God and He has never let me down. I continue to thank Him for the Mission and especially thank Him for my adopted mom, Robin, Miss Barb (Fleming), and Brenda (Nuby).

Chapter 17
Branching Beyond

Historically this ministry has stood as the northernmost rescue mission in eastern Michigan. Then in 1995 a local pastor in Alpena established a ministry called the Cornerstone Shelter. Once the ministry was underway, Ken Streeter came alongside founder Rev. Troy Baxter and served on the Board of Directors from 1998 to 2001. During this time Ken assisted the new ministry in claiming the name of Sunrise Mission and joining the Association of Gospel Rescue Missions. He helped develop the Mission's network of supporters and also kept their books for a couple of years. Today John Ritter is doing a fine job as Mission Director.

In the summer of 2001, representatives of several Bay area agencies asked for the help of the Saginaw Rescue Mission in establishing a similar outreach in Bay City. Ironically, the opportunity began developing right around the time of the September 11 attacks on America. As a result, support for the Mission's existing operations plummeted. Nonetheless, it became clear that it was God at work in preparing to open the door for a new mission in this neighboring community just to our north.

"We began to look for available buildings and soon discovered the old Samaritan Hospital," explained Mission Director Ken Streeter. "Plans proceeded and we found a very charitable spirit in friends at Bay Medical Center who owned the building." Renovations to the building and the first year of operating expenses called for a budget of 1.1 million dollars.

A staff and Board of Directors were soon organized. Naturally, it would be important to open the doors in a timely manner. However, it would be even more vital that everything be done to assure that they remain open once the work commenced. By the spring of 2003, support for the Saginaw work was recovering. By the fall, gifts and pledges for Bay City totaled $461,000. It would take another year to fulfill the campaign budget but the Good Samaritan Rescue Mission opened on March 25th, 2005.

Epilogue

Ken Streeter

I cannot sufficiently express my appreciation to Gary Warner for the outstanding work he has done in researching the history of the City Rescue Mission of Saginaw, and recording it in this milestone publication. Gary is one of many unsung heroes who, through the years, have given generously and selflessly to make the Mission what it is today. I don't need to tell the reader of his enthusiasm because it shows on every single page.

I only wish I could add the names of hundreds of staff members who have been part of the ministry through the years because they are the real story of the Saginaw Rescue Mission. I think of the heart of Jessie Fellows, who worked alongside the Hinkins. She was willing to move out of her own home and into a small apartment so that a large family who had been burned out of their home could live in hers. I never knew Jessie, but her story has etched a place in my heart, and she will always be remembered as the ultimate mission worker to me.

We also need to recognize the thousands of volunteers who have joined forces with Mission staff to demonstrate the love of Christ. Somehow Mission clients and Community Village residents reserve their deepest respect for the friends who give of their time without remuneration. Volunteered hours surely reach beyond a million at this centennial milestone. They began with folks who went through our town ministering from the Gospel Wagon in the early years, they continued with the many people who came to the Mission several nights a week during the Depression years to prepare meals for those in need, and they continue today with physicians, dentists, photographers, ministers, musicians and two hundred other job descriptions that we plan to have posted on our website **(www.rescuesaginaw.org)** by November 11, 2005 (the actual date of our centennial).

Other faithful friends that have been so important are the sponsors and stewards who have given generously from day one. I remember reading about coal vendors and coffee purveyors who donated product in the first year of the Mission's operation. I remember our friends at the Harvey Randall Wickes Foundation, the Frank Andersen Foundation, the Gerstacker and Dow Foundations in Midland, and the Citizen's Bank Trust Department (formerly Second National Bank) that have all helped so liberally through the years with grants toward major capital improvements. But I am also mindful of great friends who have come alongside and given cheerfully so that others might find hope in Christ.

I have found great joy in being a part of this ministry for over 30 years, and if the Lord allows I look forward to many more years of even more exciting work. We have a city with great needs, probably none more pressing than overcoming disenfranchisement and poverty. The next 100 years, if the Lord permits, will require new approaches to ministry. We plan to begin with a new name: **"Rescue Ministries of Mid-Michigan"** because it better represents the extension of our outreach to Bay City and …. But we also need some approaches that will undoubtedly include a more entrepreneurial focus in helping our

Discipleship Program graduates attain experience
in real work, and assistance with acquiring
automobiles and homes.

We also realize the great need in our Christian
community for multicultural churches. The
Mission is wonderfully positioned to help build
this bridge because we provide a splendid meeting
place for people from all ethnic backgrounds to
safely work together in a way that must surely
please our Lord.

It is my prayer that the reader of this little
epistle will be encouraged by the record of the
Mission's ministry over the past 100 years and join
with us in this celebration of our Double Jubilee. I
am more convinced than ever that there is no
better way to serve the King of Kings than to join
in with a ministry like that of the Rescue Mission
which seeks to lift the fallen, restore the broken,
and assist frail elders in the name of Jesus.

How To Assist a Needy Person
When You Encounter One
(And feel good about doing the right thing)

1. Be ready to share the kindness and hope of Christ, yet guard the safety of you and your family.

2. Don't hand out money. Experience has invariably shown it to be a mistake. Even though they convincingly assure you that they need it for food, it usually ends up squandered on alcohol or drugs. This isn't cynicism, just prudent caution. Take care however, not to express doubt about their honesty.

3. Always keep the Rescue Mission in mind as the place to refer a person in need of food and safe, clean shelter. Urge and direct them there. They will be treated with compassion and dignity. If they decline, offer them the McDonald's, or similar restaurant gift card that you have already made a point of keeping at hand. Everybody has to eat some time.

Succession of Superintendents

George W. Trotter 1905-1908
> (Dan W. Bush, Assistant; Ray A. Bird, Assistant)

Ira Eldridge 1908-1910

Rev. Robert A. Allen 1910; 1915

George Dibble (Lura Ellen) 1912 -
> (Fred Davis, Assistant)

William B. Kellogg 1913

Sidney Catherman 1914

(John DeFore – acting superintendent)

Fred B. Davis (Jennie) 1917

Vance Shober 1918

(John DeFore - interim sup't)

Rev. Edwin Ford

Rev. Robert. A. Allen 1921-

Rev. Horace W. "Bob" Ingersoll (Nellie) 1923-24

Walter W. Dees 1925

James Daubney (Florence) 1926 - c.1937-8

Florence Daubney 1938-1941
> ("John" Graham, Assistant Sup't)

James A. "John" Graham 1941-1942

Rev. Thomas J. Hinkin 1942-1954
> (Mrs. T. J. (Susie) Hinkin, Director of Women's Activities;
> Rev. John Erskine, Assistant Sup't;
> Miss Jessie Fellows, Home Missionary;
> William E. Bowman, Assistant Sup't - 1954)

William E. Bowman 1955

Rev. Perry L. Oden 1955 - 1956

Rev. Gerrit J. Jager (Mary) 1957-1959

Rev. Donald L. Price (Lydia) 1960 -1966

Rev. Ralph A. Brooker 1966 -1969

Thomas C. Cousineau (Madelyn) 1969-1976

Kenneth R. Streeter (Karen) 1976 -

1905 Board of Directors

Officers

A. C. White	President
N. Merriam	Vice-President
E. W. Glynn	Treasurer
J. W. Johnson	Secretary

Directors

Rev. W. A. Biss	Mrs. W. L. Hood
F. H. Bliss	Rev. Emil E. Montanus
John W. Clark	Dr. W. P. Morgan
Riley L. Crane	Hamilton Watson
George W. Trotter	

2005 Board of Directors

Officers

William E. Severance	President
Les L. Miller	Vice-President
Melissa L. Cabine	Secretary
Frank W. Vaydik	Treasurer
Kenneth R. Streeter	Executive Director

Directors

Shirley Bidwell	Carole L. Hemminger
Dr. Clyde P. Davenport	John W. Nagy
James Fleming	Ruth Anne Rye
Martha S. Haenlein-Boese	Curtis R. Thayer
Kenneth M. Hasse	Dale E. Wieck

Honorary Life Member

Carl Lichtenwald

STATE OF MICHIGAN

SPECIAL TRIBUTE

To

THE CITY RESCUE MISSION OF SAGINAW
100 Years of Service to the Community!

LET IT BE KNOWN, That it is a distinct pleasure and privilege to honor and commend the **City Rescue Mission of Saginaw** upon the celebration of its 100th anniversary. Since 1905, the **City Rescue Mission** has provided emergency assistance to men, women, and children from all walks of life during their times of need. We admire and applaud this faith-based organization for its service to the community over the last 100 years!

The **City Rescue Mission of Saginaw** provides numerous services for those facing adversity, including shelter, meals and clothing for the homeless, counseling for substance abusers, assisted living for seniors, and job training. Most importantly, the **City Rescue Mission** aims to glorify God by helping people in need, with an ultimate goal of directing individuals toward a more productive life through the teachings of Christ.

This wonderful nonprofit organization is made up of a thirteen-member Board of Directors, who are selected to represent a variety of denominational and vocational perspectives. Police, government agencies, churches and residents of Mid-Michigan can be confident that if they refer a person to the **City Rescue Mission**, that individual will be met with a compassionate and highly-professional staff who are dedicated to improving lives and spreading the Gospel of Christ.

IN SPECIAL TRIBUTE, Therefore, This official document is signed and dedicated to congratulate and commend the **City Rescue Mission of Saginaw** on its 100th anniversary celebration. May this Godly organization continue to offer compassion and care to the disadvantaged for many years to come.

Mike Goschka, State Senator
32nd District

Roger Kahn, M.D., State Representative
94th District

John Moolenaar, State Representative
98th District

The Ninety-Third Legislature
At Lansing
August 23, 2005

STATE OF MICHIGAN

SPECIAL TRIBUTE

To

THE CITY RESCUE MISSION OF SAGINAW, INC

LET IT BE KNOWN, That it is with deep appreciation of the significance of this milestone that we commend the management and staff of The City Rescue Mission of Saginaw, Inc. as they mark the 100th anniversary of the founding of this exemplary name. We are proud to recognize the important role that this business has played in contributing to both the economic well-being of the area and the lives of countless citizens.

The City Rescue Mission of Saginaw, Inc. was founded in 1905 be Mel Trotter. Mel Trotter and a concerned group of Christians saw an opportunity to minister to "the fallen" and converted a saloon into a place of hope. Since then it has become a vital element in helping Michigan grow and adapt to needs in commerce and all aspects of life in Saginaw. This success in maintaining competitiveness during an era of many challenges is the direct result of the commitment of the people of this business and their ability to work together to offer the best services over the years. Even as our cyclical Michigan economy has presented obstacles to growth and stability, The City Rescue Mission of Saginaw has sustained itself through dedication and innovation.

In looking back over 100 years of The City Rescue Mission of Saginaw's history, it is clear that this name has set its course with a continuing look to the future. While the changes of the marketplace dictate many of the decisions for any good business, The City Rescue Mission of Saginaw has also demonstrated the importance of providing shelter and supportive services for the homeless persons. We are grateful for all that The City Rescue Mission has contributed to Saginaw and all of Michigan.

IN SPECIAL TRIBUTE, Therefore, This document is signed and dedicated to commemorate the 100th anniversary of The City Rescue Mission of Saginaw, Inc. We salute the management and staff on this happy occasion and wish them well in the years to come.

Carl M. Williams, State Representative
The Ninety-Fifth District

Jennifer M. Granholm
Governor

The Ninety-Third Legislature
At Lansing
Tuesday, August 23, 2005

Bibliography

Chapter 1: To the Rescue – *Who are the needy?*

1. Hertel, Leona. *Man With A Mission: Mel Trotter and His Legacy for the Rescue Mission Movement.* Grand Rapids, MI: Kregel Publications, 2000: 17.

Chapter 2: The Birth of a Phenomenon

1. Nasmith, David. First annual report of the Glasgow (Scotland) City Mission, 1827.

2. History: "The Roots of New York City Rescue Mission." www.nycrescue.org

3. "The History of Pacific Garden Mission." www.pgm.org

Chapter 3: Rescue's Champion

1. Hertel, Leona. *Man With A Mission: Mel Trotter and His Legacy for the Rescue Mission Movement.* Grand Rapids, MI: Kregel Publications, 2000: 17.

2. Ibid.

3. Preacher Biographies: "Mel Trotter" www.swordofthelord.com

4. Trotter, Melvin E. *These Forty Years.* London, UK: Marshall, Morgan & Scott, Ltd., 1939: vii.

5. Ibid: 55.

6. Ibid: 38.

Chapter 4: A *Wide-Open* Opportunity

1. Gross, Stuart. *Saginaw, A History of the Land and the City.* Woodland Hills, CA: Windsor Publications, 1980: 25.

2. Kilar, Jeremy W. *Saginaw's Changeable Past: An Illustrated History.* St. Louis, MO: G. Bradley Publishing, 1994: 75.

3. Gross, Stuart. *Frankie and the Barons.* Fowlerville, MI: Wilderness Adventure Books, 1991: 106.

4. "Rescue Mission Opens Tonight." *The Saginaw Evening News* 11 Nov.1905: 11.

Chapter 5: Ripe for Rescue

1. Handlin, Oscar. "History of the United States." *The World Book Encyclopedia.* Chicago: World Book-Childcraft International, 1980: Vol. 20: 115.

2. Kilar, Jeremy W. *Saginaw's Changeable Past: An Illustrated History.* St. Louis, MO: G. Bradley Publishing, 1994: 127.

3. "Rescue Mission Opens Tonight." *The Saginaw Evening News* 11 Nov.1905: 11.

4. Trotter, Melvin E. *These Forty Years.* London, UK: Marshall, Morgan & Scott, Ltd., 1939: 17.

5. Ibid: 38.

6. "Everything Ready For Rescue Mission." *The Saginaw Evening News* 12 Oct. 1907.

7. "California Gets George W. Trotter." *The Saginaw Evening News* 3 April 1908.

8. *Saginaw Directory 1908:* R. L. Polk & Co.

9. "Rescue Mission Was Overflowed." *The Saginaw Evening News* 24 March 1906:10.

10. Trotter, Melvin E. *These Forty Years.* London, UK: Marshall, Morgan & Scott, Ltd., 1939: 38.

11. "Everything Ready For Rescue Mission." *The Saginaw Evening News* 12 Oct. 1907.

Chapter 6: To the Byways – *Meeting Human Need in the Name of Jesus*

1. "Rescue Mission Annual Meeting." *The Saginaw Evening News* 29 Oct. 1906.

2. Trotter, Melvin E. *These Forty Years.* London, UK: Marshall, Morgan & Scott, Ltd., 1939: 38.

3. *Second Annual Report of the City Rescue Mission - Saginaw, MI.* 1906-1907: 17; Mills, James Cooke. *History of Saginaw County.* Saginaw: Seemann and Peters, 1918: 360.

4. "City Rescue Mission to Observe Ninth Anniversary With Special Meeting in Auditorium on Sunday." *The Saginaw Daily News* 24 Oct. 1914: 7.

Chapter 7: Lifting the Fallen

1. "Rescue Mission Was Overflowed." *The Saginaw Evening News* 24 March 1906: 10.

2. Gross, Stuart. *Frankie and the Barons.* Fowlerville, MI: Wilderness Adventure Books, 1991: 57.

3. Trotter, Melvin E. *These Forty Years.* London, UK: Marshall, Morgan & Scott, Ltd., 1939: 37.

4. "Rescue Mission Annual Meeting." *The Saginaw Evening News* 29 Oct. 1906.

Chapter 8: The Gospel Wagon

1. "The History of Pacific Garden Mission." www.pgm.org.

2. "Gospel Wagon To Start Out Today." *The Saginaw Courier-Herald* 15 July 1906.

3. "The History of Pacific Garden Mission." www.pgm.org.

4. Ellis, William T. *"Billy Sunday," The Man and His Message.* Chicago: Moody Press, 1959: 32.

5. Burger, Delores T. *Women Who Changed the Heart of the City.* Grand Rapids, MI: Kregel Publications, 1997.

6. "An Illustrated And Commercial Review of Saginaw, Michigan." New York: *The New York Industrial Recorder,* 1906: 7.

7. "Gospel Wagon To Start Out Today." *The Saginaw Courier-Herald* 15 July 1906.

8. Ibid; "Rescue Mission Echoes" *Union and City Rescue Missions – Los Angeles, CA 1909-1910 - Fourth Annual Report: 3.*

9. "Rescue Mission Annual Meeting." *The Saginaw Evening News* 29 Oct. 1906; *Second Annual Report of the City Rescue Mission - Saginaw, MI* 1906-1907: 8.

Chapter 9: Reaching Further

1. "Gospel Wagon To Start Out Today." *The Saginaw Courier-Herald* 15 July 1906.

2. *Second Annual Report of the City Rescue Mission - Saginaw, MI* 1906-1907: 8.

3. "Interesting Service At The Rescue Mission." *The Saginaw Evening News* 7 Nov. 1908.

4. "Annual Meeting Of The Rescue Mission." *The Saginaw Courier-Herald* 11 Oct. 1911.

5. Ibid; "Interesting Service At The Rescue Mission." *The Saginaw Evening News* 7 Nov. 1908.

6. Ibid.

7. "City Rescue Mission to Observe Ninth Anniversary With Special Meeting in Auditorium on Sunday." *The Saginaw Daily News* 24 Oct. 1914: 7.

8. "Saginaw City Rescue Mission Women's Sewing Society." *The Saginaw Daily News* circa 1930.

9. "Annual Meeting Of Rescue Mission." *The Saginaw Evening News* 10 Oct. 1908: 5

10. "Everything Ready For Rescue Mission." *The Saginaw Evening News* 12 Oct. 1907.

11. "Annual Meeting Of Rescue Mission."
The Saginaw Evening News 30 Oct. 1909.

12. "Interior Changes Made In Mission."
The Saginaw Daily News 11 Oct. 1911: 9.

13. "Farewell For Supt. Trotter." *The Saginaw
Evening News* 30 April 1908.

14. "Annual Meeting Of Rescue Mission."
The Saginaw Evening News 10 Oct. 1908: 5.

15. Ibid.

16. *Second Annual Report of the City Rescue Mission
- Saginaw, MI* 1906-1907: 11.

17. "City Rescue Mission to Observe Ninth
Anniversary With Special Meeting in Auditorium
on Sunday." *The Saginaw Daily News* 24 Oct. 1914: 7.

Chapter 10: Movements of Progress

1. "Gives All Kinds of Relief." *The Saginaw Daily
News* 21 Sept. 1932:

2. "Rescue Mission To Hold Fifth Annual."
The Saginaw Daily News 22 Oct. 1910.

3. "Rescue Mission To Move November 1."
The Saginaw Daily News 21 Oct. 1911.

4. "Interior Changes Made In Mission." *The
Saginaw Daily News* 11 Oct. 1911: 9.

5. Trotter, Melvin E. *These Forty Years.* London,
UK: Marshall, Morgan & Scott, Ltd., 1939: 41.

6. "Rescue Mission To Hold Fifth Annual." *The Saginaw Daily News* 22 Oct. 1910; "Rev. Allen Returns To Rescue Mission." *The Saginaw News Courier* 2 Oct. 1921.

7. "Rescue Mission To Hold Fifth Annual." *The Saginaw Daily News* 22 Oct. 1910; "Rescue Mission." *The Saginaw Courier-Herald* 1 Oct. 1911; "Rescue Mission Annual Is Held." *The Saginaw Daily News* 30 Sept. 1912; *Saginaw Directory 1913:* R. L. Polk & Co.; *Saginaw Directory 1914:* R. L. Polk & Co.

8. "Do Your Best; Leave Rest to God." *The Saginaw Sunday News* 15 May 1932.

9. "Civic Leaders Honor Pastor." *The Saginaw News* 2 March 1938.

10. "City Rescue Mission to Celebrate Fourteenth Anniversary Next Week." *The Saginaw News Courier* 15 Sept. 1918.

11. Huthmacher, J. Joseph. "Prohibition." *The World Book Encyclopedia.* Chicago: World Book-Childcraft International, 1980: Vol. 15: 718.

12. "Rev. Allen Returns To Rescue Mission." *The Saginaw News Courier* 2 Oct. 1921.

13. Obituary: "Ingersoll, Rev. H. W. (Bob), Prudenville, MI" *The Saginaw News* 16 Feb. 1966.

14. Hertel, Leona. *Man With A Mission: Mel Trotter and His Legacy for the Rescue Mission Movement.* Grand Rapids, MI: Kregel Publications, 2000: 92.

15. Trotter, Melvin E. *These Forty Years.* London, UK: Marshall, Morgan & Scott, Ltd., 1939: 42.

16. "Birthday Greetings To Bill Birdsall." *The Saginaw Rescue Mission – Newsletter* Summer 1982: 4.

17. *The Guiding Light* – Official Publication of the City Rescue Mission - March 1964, Vol. 7, No. 3: 1.

18. "Chance Led Him to Mission Work." *The Saginaw Sunday News* 30 Oct. 1932.

19. Display Ad. *The Saginaw News Courier* 13 March 1926: 3.

Chapter 11: Increasing Vigil
Through The Long Dark Night

1. "Gives All Kinds of Relief." *The Saginaw Daily News* 21 Sept. 1932.

2. "Mission Expanding Services To Needy." *The Saginaw News Courier* 23 July 1926.

3. Trotter, Melvin E. *These Forty Years.* London, U.K.: Marshall, Morgan & Scott, Ltd., 1939: 31.

4. Shannon, David A. "Great Depression." *The World Book Encyclopedia.* Chicago: World Book-Childcraft International, 1980: Vol. 8, 340c.

5. Gross, Stuart. *Saginaw, A History of the Land and the City.* Woodland Hills, CA: Windsor Publications, 1980: 101.

6. Shannon, David A. "Great Depression." *The World Book Encyclopedia.* Chicago: World Book-Childcraft International, 1980: Vol. 8, 340c.

7. "Serving the City's Hungry, the Tired and the Destitute." *The Saginaw Daily News* 22 Dec. 1935.
8. "Hobo Activity Picking Up, Check Reveals." *The Saginaw News* 5 July 1949.

9. "Reports of Mission Show Improvement in Employment Here." *The Saginaw Daily News* 18 Oct. 1930.

10. *Webster's New World Dictionary of the American Language.* College Edition. Cleveland; New York: The World Publishing Company, 1968: 690. "Hobo Activity Picking Up, Check Reveals." *The Saginaw News* 5 July 1949.

11. "Rescue Mission Crowded, Barn Would Be Big Help." *The Saginaw Sunday News* 6 March 1932.

12. "Mission Gets Larger Home." The Saginaw Daily News 22 Nov. 1932: 1.

13. "Mission To Add To Its Building." The Saginaw Sunday News 2 Dec. 1934; "Serving the City's Hungry, the Tired and the Destitute." *The Saginaw Daily News* 22 Dec. 1935.

14. Ibid.

15. Ibid; "1931 Report - Saginaw City Rescue Mission To Study Relativity - The "Einstein Theory."

16. "Let's Get Acquainted." City Rescue Mission, 1941.

17. "Mission's Rolling Kitchen Boon to Homeless Negroes." *The Saginaw News* 3 March 1940.

18. "Many A Person Gets Break At Rescue Mission." *The Saginaw News* 23 Oct. 1938.

19. *The Mission Messenger* 1947: Issue published unidentified.

Chapter 12: Changing Times

1. "Assistant Is Appointed For City Rescue Mission." *The Saginaw News* 19 Oct. 1943.

2. Slominski, Betty. Pastor's Profile—"Dreamed Of Baseball, Or Career On Stage." *The Saginaw News* 15 Aug. 1953: 2.

3. "Hobo Activity Picking Up, Check Reveals." *The Saginaw News* 5 July 1949.

4. Ibid.

5. Ibid.

6. "Mrs. Hinkin Keeps Busy In Rescue Mission Work." *The Saginaw News* circa 1951.

7. "Mission Aides." *The Saginaw News* 11 Oct. 1951.

8. "Rescue Mission's Auxiliary Elects." *The Saginaw News* 18 Nov. 1951.

9. "Its Doors Are Always Open, There's Hope Inside." *The Saginaw News* 23 Nov. 1952.

10. "Rev. T. J. Hinkin Claimed By Death." *The Saginaw News* 24 Dec. 1954.

11. "W. E. Bowman." *The Saginaw News* 7 Jan. 1955.

12. "New Superintendent At Rescue Mission." *The Saginaw News* 17 Sept. 1955.

13. "City Rescue Mission Head Departing For Ohio Post." *The Saginaw News* 1 Dec. 1959.

14. *"Unshackled!"* "The Don Price Story" Chicago: Pacific Garden Mission, 1981.

15. Hertel, Leona. *Man With A Mission: Mel Trotter and His Legacy for the Rescue Mission Movement.* Grand Rapids, MI: Kregel Publications, 2000: 104.

16. "Mission Names New Director." *The Saginaw News* 1 Sept. 1966.

17. "City Rescue Mission To Become Faith Mission Jan. 1." *The Saginaw News* 13 Dec. 1969: 1.

18. "Superintendent Is Named at Mission." The Saginaw News 1 Nov. 1969; "Head of Rescue Mission quits." *The Saginaw News* 16 Oct. 1976.

Chapter 14: The New Face of Homelessness

1. *Intercessors for America Newsletter* 1 Feb. 1985.

2. 1984 Study. U.S. Department of Housing and Urban Development.

3. Cahan, Vicky. "The Feminization of Poverty: More Women Are Getting Poorer." *Business Week* 28 Jan. 1985.

4. Ibid.

5. 1984 Study. U.S. Department of Housing and Urban Development.

6. "Family Shelter Overcrowded, Underfunded." *YOUR NEWSLETTER FROM The Saginaw Rescue Mission* Jan/Feb 1996: 1; "1995 Snapshot Survey of the Homeless." International Union of Gospel Missions (IUGM).

Chapter 16: Preparing the Way Ahead

1. 1996 Report. National Coalition for the Homeless.